CHIROPRACTIC MARKETING TOOLS THAT WILL ABSOLUTELY GROW YOUR PRACTICE

Dr. John Reizer

Copyright © Dr. John Reizer 2008 (First Edition)
Copyright © Dr. John Reizer 2019 (Second Edition)

Portions of this book appeared in the following publications: "Up and Running-Opening a Chiropractic Office" © Drs. John & Steven Reizer 2002 "Teaching Your Patients Chiropractic" © Dr. John Reizer 2006 "15 Secrets to Becoming a Successful Chiropractor" © Dr. John Reizer 2005 "Waist Away: How I Lost 70 Pounds in 7 Months Without Drugs or Surgery" © Dr. John Reizer 2008

All Rights Reserved. Printed in the United States of America
No part of this publication may be reproduced, stored in a retrieval system, or transmitted, in any form or by any means electronic, mechanical, photocopying, recording, or otherwise, without the prior written permission of the author.

ISBN# 9781095939130

Published By Amazon.com

About The Author

Dr. John Reizer is a 1986 magna cum laude graduate of Sherman College of Chiropractic. Born in Lakewood, New Jersey in 1963, he is a former associate professor of clinical sciences at Sherman College. John privately practices in Boiling Springs, South Carolina. More information is available at www.johnreizer.com.

Disclaimer

The information that has been written in this book is based upon the opinions of the author. The author accepts no liability or responsibility whatsoever either directly or indirectly from the use of any of the concepts/information printed inside this publication.

Introduction

This book has only one purpose which is to help doctors of chiropractic properly market their professional services to prospective patients. Whether you have been a practicing doctor for many years or you have just recently opened your doors for the very first time, it is imperative that you learn how to package and present your product to potential patients in an intelligent manner.

Properly marketing chiropractic services can be a challenging proposition for many young and established doctors. Practitioners often find out, through trial and error scenarios, that a particular strategy which might seem to be logical and work very well in one type of business climate does not always bode well in the boundaries of another.

After practicing chiropractic for over 21 years in a private practice setting, and spending over 10 years as an associate professor of clinical sciences at Sherman College of Straight Chiropractic, I feel that I have finally figured out some absolutely sure-fire ways to cost effectively market my professional services to the members of various communities. It is my desire to share these marketing concepts with my readers.

One classic mistake that doctors will often make when operating a practice is to foolishly spend excessive amounts of hard earned money on marketing techniques that will ultimately yield substandard results. Because many chiropractors lack the business skills that are required to successfully market professional chiropractic services, they incorrectly make the assumption that it is necessary to overspend on various marketing campaigns in an effort to generate a healthy supply of new patients for their practices.

Throughout the many years that I have been involved with this profession, I have been trying to study the various ingredients that make chiropractic marketing efforts successful. In many instances, there are only subtle differences between strategies that will deliver fantastic versus mediocre results. I firmly believe that excellent results, demonstrated by a regular influx of new and reactivated patients in a given practice setting, acquired through a well thought out marketing plan is something that every business owner should strive for. If a doctor lacks the skills which are necessary to create an intelligent marketing plan, he or she should take a trip to the local library and check out some publications that discuss basic marketing procedures. A basic understanding of marketing a business will be helpful to any chiropractor launching a new business or trying to pump energy into an already existing model.

Knowing about the basics in any genre of study is vital if one wishes to achieve higher levels of success within the same discipline at a later date. In the case of marketing a chiropractic business, entrepreneurs will need to become cognizant of the fact that some modifications will need to be made to some of the classic marketing techniques that have been tested over time and revered by the so called experts. As sound as many of these principles might be when used in other categories of business, readers must be aware that a chiropractic practice, in some respects, represents a completely different animal. A chiropractic business can be very similar in some ways to many functioning businesses, and then again it can be very different in other ways when compared to conventional business prototypes. The reason for this fact is because there is an obvious difference between the mindset of the American consumer and the American healthcare consumer.

Healthcare consumers usually think and operate slightly different than traditional consumers. When people wear their "healthcare consumer hats", they almost always analyze situations using a different formula than they would if they were dealing with non healthcare issues. For example, consumers would probably rarely choose to eat at only specifically selected dining establishments that had been pre-approved by insurance companies. Most people would not put up with this type of restricted access. They would gladly pay "out of pocket" the extra money to dine at a restaurant of their own choosing. The same hypothesis however, cannot be used when it is applied to healthcare consumers who might be shopping for the services of a chiropractor. If these prospective patients were shopping for chiropractic services, and had insurance plans that limited their access to specifically selected insurance doctors, it is highly unlikely that any of these healthcare consumers would pay "out of pocket" expenses to a specific provider residing outside the confines of the well defined insurance network. People have a completely different mindset when it comes to purchasing a sandwich versus a chiropractic service.

    In this book I have written about extremely cost effective chiropractic marketing tools that will help you grow your practice. I believe any chiropractors that make an honest effort to implement these marketing concepts into their practices will see a drastic increase in the number of new patients they will attract. I also believe that many of these marketing ideas will gradually, over time, help convince a large number of your inactive patients to reactivate. In this way you will get the maximum results desired from your marketing program which will ultimately help you to see a higher volume of patients. This will eventually allow you to help many more people in your community that would otherwise not have access to your valuable professional services.

- Dr. John Reizer

Business Cards

Business cards are one of the most cost effective ways to market a chiropractic business. They are obviously one of the best marketing tools you can purchase for your practice and yet most chiropractic entrepreneurs will completely overlook their importance while simultaneously underestimating their potential to positively impact the level of patient growth in the practice setting. There are a number of good companies that exist in the market place that will allow you to create a high quality product for your business at a very nominal charge.

Business cards are easy to produce, easy to store and most importantly very easy to carry on your person at all times. The more of these cards you give out, the more visible your practice becomes. Never be shy about giving out business cards in an effort to market your practice. When you go out to dinner always be sure to leave behind your card. Whenever you attend networking functions of any sort you should take with you an ample supply of cards. Remember that business cards are like seeds in a garden. The more of them you plant the better the chances will be that your patient volume will grow.

Designing Your Card

Your business card should include your trade name, the chiropractor's name, phone number, fax number, address, office hours and some professional services that you may provide. In addition, a logo can be placed on the card to identify your profession.

Reizer Chiropractic Center

Dr. John L. Reizer

188 Blalock Road

Boiling Springs, SC 29316

Phone: 864-494-0121

Hours by Appointment   Affordable Care for
                    the Entire Family

When designing your card it is also important to keep your word count to a minimum. You certainly want to provide prospects with enough vital information about your business, but on the other hand you never want to make the card too busy with excess content. Instead, you should try to create a simple yet very pleasing to look at product that attempts to get your unique company message out to the general community.

Another important item to remember is to keep the font on your business card at a reasonable size that is easy for most people to read. I have witnessed on many occasions business cards that have featured very small print which makes me not want to look at the card. Sometimes the print is large enough to read but the color schemes that have been chosen make the card a difficult view. A lot of careful thought and consideration should go into the general design of your product. Do not just throw the document together without taking the time to think about what you are trying to achieve.

It is equally important to make sure that your card stands apart from other competitors. Try to remember that your primary goal is to make your business card grab the attention of prospective patients. Although it might be an easy task to get your card into the hands of a prospect, it is a much bigger challenge to try and keep those potential patients from tossing your marketing masterpiece into a garbage can or perhaps filing it into a drawer where it will never be seen again by human eyes. You might also consider making your cards magnets so that patients can stick them on a refrigerator or some other kitchen appliance that is always in a visible location.

When purchasing business cards, it's advisable to select high quality paper products; certainly ones that convey a truly professional image. Each time you pass out your card, you're handing the prospect your professional signature which is a direct reflection of your professional image. If your card looks like it has been produced on flimsy or cheap looking paper or if the general appearance of your card looks unprofessional, people will make a mental note of this fact and will be more likely to judge you and your practice negatively.

Proofread Your Work

Although this is common sense, remember to proofread your finished product before you authorize the initial order. You can save yourself a lot of headaches, additional expenses and extra frustration by making sure that everything is suitable to print and that the final proof is free of errors.

Make Your Cards Work for You!

I absolutely believe that it is important to make your business cards work for you and this cannot be accomplished by leaving them stored in the box they were shipped in. Take your business cards everywhere you go and be sure to place them on bulletin boards in super markets, leave them at the schools your kids go to when doing health talks and leave them in the local libraries when scheduling health seminars for the people in your community.

You should also make a genuine effort to visit each business owner in your town. Tell each owner that you are new to the area and that you would appreciate any advice he or she might have to offer about running a business in the community. Exchange business cards with this person and write down important information that you talked about on the back of the person's card. Later on you will review your notes and you will write a personalized letter to each individual thanking him or her for any advice that might have been offered. You should also take the time to invite each business owner to come visit you at your business location. You will repeat this process for every business owner that you meet in your community. This is how you get yourself known in a community, and the exchanging of business cards is a very useful way to accomplish this important exercise.

Another neat thing you can do with a business card is to print a coupon on the back side of the card. I would place an expiration date on the offer of approximately one month. You would be absolutely amazed at the number of new patients I have picked up throughout my career just by passing out a business card with a hand printed coupon on the reverse side.

Companies to Choose From

The companies listed below will help you to design and deliver a very professional business card at a nominal fee, and in some cases for no charge at all. The only fee that you might incur is a shipping charge. If you select a slow mode of shipping your expense will be limited to a few dollars.

| VISTA PRINT (vistaprint.com) |
| Free Business Card Printers (freebusinesscardprinters.com) |
| Free Printable Business Cards (freeprintablebusinesscards.net) |

Newsletters

Newsletters are a great marketing tool for any business and they are especially useful in marketing a chiropractic business. When you create and publish your own office newsletter, you literally create a forum to talk about absolutely anything you want. One of the main reasons I like to use newsletters is because they allow me the chance to reach my patients in their homes on a regular basis. The benefits associated with the regular distribution of newsletters are endless. Not only do I get a chance to educate my patients with these informative publications, but I am also afforded an opportunity to run a most important and very effective marketing program at the same time. Newsletters will keep your name, office, and chiropractic in front of patients and on their minds even when they are not in your office. The simple fact that a newsletter can accomplish this feat makes it virtually a priceless marketing tool.

The timing of your newsletter is extremely important. I recommend a monthly publication. Other consultants may endorse bi-monthly or quarterly circulation, but I strongly disagree. When you think of the various forms of propaganda and anti-chiropractic marketing campaigns that flood the television stations as well as other media outlets on a daily basis, it is hard to make the case that less distribution is better. In addition, when your practice is young or your already established practice is looking for continued growth, you want to be able to reach as many patients as you can, and you want to be able to do this as often as possible. The monthly newsletter is one of the best ways to accomplish this.

Commit to this project right now, but realize that once you start doing a newsletter you must keep producing it every month. This is not an effective tool if it is done haphazardly and at irregular intervals. However, when you commit to a regular schedule and your newsletter arrives at the first of the month, every month; prospects, patients and any other readers will begin to take notice. Your audience will begin to anticipate its arrival. Patients who may not have been in for some time will suddenly show up at your office. Keep in mind that you may only get to spend anywhere from five to fifteen minutes an office visit with each patient. A well constructed newsletter gives you the opportunity to spend additional time with patients outside of your office.

What Should You Write About?

What should you write about in your newsletters? Anything you want! Keep it chiropractic, of course. This is your forum, your soap box. Use this vehicle to market your professional services to your entire practice and to as many prospects as possible. You can educate patients on any topic in chiropractic that you desire. For example, you might want to create an article that will explain some of the terminology that the profession commonly uses. You might also want to teach about the concepts of Innate Intelligence, herniated discs, osteoarthritis, rheumatoid arthritis, wellness care, subluxations as well as a multitude of other important topics. Write an article about symptoms as indicators of health status. You can also write about the need for regular care and about the phases of subluxation degeneration in the spinal column. Break down each section of your health talk and expand them into a series of articles. At least one article of your newsletter should be purely educational. Other topics you can write about include patient testimonials, happenings in your office (in office promotions), healthy living tips, healthy recipes, etc. The important thing to remember is to use your imagination and be creative. The possibilities are endless.

Newsletters Are Inexpensive to Produce

A newsletter is a very inexpensive way to educate your patients. You do not need a fancy four-page product with glossy paper and accompanying photographs to send out an effective newsletter. A simple one page, 8 ½" x 11" paper printed on both sides can be quite effective. Almost any desktop publishing software program will have newsletter templates that you can follow in order to create your own personal publication. Pick a design and a look for your newsletter and get started. Give your newsletter a catchy title and be sure that all of your office contact information is included as well. After you have written your newsletter, you will only need to print one master copy. Take the master copy to any office supply store and for about three cents you can print as many as you need. Stick the newsletters in envelopes and get them in the mail. It is just that simple.

Another very good idea is to print extra copies of your newsletter beyond the number which you will mail out. Keep the extras on hand in your office for patients to take home so they can give them out to their friends. Take additional copies and drop them off at a local gym or health food store which you frequent on a regular basis. You should also include a monthly calendar with each newsletter that informs patients of office closings, holidays, in office promotions, etc. Sure, this is an extra page of paper to print each month, but most patients will take the calendar with your office name, office hours, and office contact information and stick it on their refrigerator every month. Talk about being in a patient's face all month long! This additional piece of paper is well worth the extra expense.

The newsletter, when used as a marketing tool, is a chiropractor's best friend. If used properly, a newsletter can help you build your business in almost no time at all.

In – Office Promotions

The idea of offering a promotional campaign within the construct of your physical office is not a new concept. Chiropractors, dentists, and probably many other healthcare professionals have regularly utilized this type of a strategy in order to attract new patients.

Most people have a competitive streak in them. Most of the patients in your practice will not be opposed to having an opportunity to take part in an in-office promotion/contest that you might decide to sponsor.

Over the many years I have practiced as a chiropractor, I have set up a good number of in-office contests for my patients. My primary goal was always to get my established patients to refer me a fresh supply of new patients. One of the easiest ways I would accomplish this was to purchase a plastic message board with a classic black background and white plastic letters. I would hang the sign in a conspicuous location in my office waiting room. The message I would place on the sign would read *"PATIENT REFERRAL CONTEST."* The objective of the contest was to see which patient could refer me the most new patients in a given month. Each time an established patient referred a new patient to my practice, I would place his or her name, along with the number of patients referred, on the sign in the waiting room. At the end of the month I would post the winner of the monthly contest on the sign as well as in the monthly newsletter that I would write. I also awarded the winner a small gift certificate to a local movie theatre or to a department store. These new patient referral contests were very well received by my practice members and the contests regularly increased the number of new patients that came to my office each month.

    A simple promotional contest can get your patients excited about referring you new patients. This is an inexpensive way to get your established patient base to promote your chiropractic business. Patients will go out of their way to build your practice if you give them a good reason to do so.

    In every contest I promoted within my office I would hand out some sort of marketing gadget for the award. It might be a shirt, magnetic calendar, pen or even a key chain. It did not matter to me what the gift was. All of the awarded gifts had one thing in common. They all had my office name and phone number printed on them. All of these items were cheap to purchase and they all helped to promote my business.

At the end of the year, I awarded the person who referred me the most new patients with a bigger prize. On one occasion I awarded a patient a cruise vacation. This was a big conversation piece amongst my established patients during the course of the year as I advertised the vacation package in my office newsletter as well as in other promotional materials that were available in the office. The actual cruise only cost me a few hundred dollars. I negotiated a business deal with a travel agency that was just a few miles down the road. I gave them some excellent exposure in my office which helped their business and they gave me a great deal on the price of the cruise. The promotion was a huge success. This one contest by itself generated well over one hundred new patients in my practice.

When constructing your own in-office promotions try to think outside the box. There are many clever ways to put these promotional campaigns into action. Select a contest that resonates with your own personality. You have to be comfortable with the program you are offering. (***In addition, make sure that you check with your state's*** *chiropractic board to see if a particular marketing campaign is legal.)*

A Press Release

Another wonderful marketing tool that is often completely overlooked by chiropractors is a press release. A press release is a written document you can create and distribute to various local and national media outlets. The reason you would send out a press release is to try and convince the people who operate the media (editors and journalists) to pick up and publish your newsworthy story.

A press release is a great way to get your company information into newspapers, search engines, television and radio spots, as well as other media reporting vehicles absolutely free of charge. In my own career as a chiropractor and author, I have written a good number of press releases in an effort to promote my professional practice or a book I was trying to market.

There is a basic formula/template you should follow when attempting to write a press release document. It is very important to follow the structured format established by various editors and journalists over the years. If you fail to prepare your press release in the generally accepted format, you will probably have a very slim chance of having the document reviewed when it is submitted. If however, you follow the proper formatting requirements, your press release will stand a very good chance of being read and published in various media circles.

When writing a press release it is a very good idea to place your company logo on the front page of your document. The first page of your press release should always contain the words **"PRESS RELEASE: FOR IMMEDIATE RELEASE"** in all capital letters. The next part of the press release that should be written is known as the title and it should be written in a very powerful style. The title of a press release needs to grab the attention of the editor or reader. After writing the title, it is sometimes considered appropriate to write a sub-title for additional impact.

The major portion of the press release is known as the "body" and should contain the meat of your news or story information. In this section you should always include the *"5 W's of Journalism Reporting."* In other words you will need to write who or what the story is about, where the story is taking place, when the news event occurred, and why it is important or newsworthy. If you have covered these five components in your press release, then you have most likely done your job properly and created a great *"body"* for your document.

The final portion of your press release should provide a synopsis of your news event along with some basic information about you or your company/product. Always finish the press release by writing in the three ### symbols. This is the professionally recognized way of ending the press release. If you omit this step your document will probably be considered unprofessional and not reviewed.

In January, 2008 I published a new book about a weight loss program I created the previous year. In the process of marketing my book, I wrote a press release which I submitted to various media outlets. I have included that press release in this section so my readers can observe how a proper press release should be prepared. I have also included a second sample press release that can be used to announce the opening of a chiropractic office.

The Waist Away Company

**Contact: Dr. John Reizer
Phone: 864-494-0121
Email: drjohnlreizer@gmail.com**

PRESS RELEASE - FOR IMMEDIATE RELEASE:

January 30, 2008

Chiropractor Writes Book Explaining How He Lost 70 Pounds Without Drugs or Surgery!
-- Chiropractor, assistant professor, and bestselling chiropractic author, Dr. John Reizer recently published a new book on how he lost 70 pounds in just 7 months. --

SPARTANBURG, SC, January 30, 2008 - Chiropractor, assistant professor, and bestselling chiropractic author, Dr. John Reizer recently published a new book on how he lost 70 pounds in just 7 months. The book, which was published on January 25, 2008 by Lulu Press, is titled appropriately, "Waist Away - How I Lost 70 Pounds in 7 Months without Drugs or Surgery."

Dr. Reizer began the arduous process of shedding 70 pounds of excess weight back on January 10, 2007. The South Carolina resident stated that he designed and perfected his own weight loss program from the knowledge he acquired while studying to become a doctor of chiropractic over 22 years ago.

"I believe that the Waist Away Program helped to accelerate my body's metabolism for extended periods of time which allowed me to regularly lose weight without hitting those annoying plateaus that so many dieters often experience," the author explained.

Reizer, who has authored four bestselling books on the subject of chiropractic over the past six years, decided to take a proactive course of action in dealing with his weight condition. His strategy was based on four simple principles of weight loss success and he claims that once he implemented these principles into his life, there was nothing that could have prevented his success.

"At the age of 44 I was classified as an obese person. I was writing bestselling books on the subject of chiropractic, and I was deeply involved in the process of educating future doctors while simultaneously giving out advice to my patients in a private practice setting. I thought to myself, *why would anyone want to take healthcare advice from someone who was obese and out of shape?* I then asked myself an even more painful question. *Would I take healthcare advice from someone who looked like me?* After thinking the question over for a few seconds the answer I came up with was - probably not. I was also extremely concerned that my health was being severely compromised by the accumulation of extra weight on my body. So I decided to do something about my problem."

"Waist Away" is the true account of how Reizer lost 70 pounds in just 7 months. He was able to attain his weight loss goal without utilizing any type of strenuous exercise program, expensive gym equipment, prepackaged food plans, dangerous drugs or surgical procedures. He was also able to eat a healthy diet and never once starved or deprived himself of any valuable nutritional requirements.

In his book, the author very clearly explains how he was able to accomplish an almost impossible task in a relatively short period of time. The collection of photographs that are in the "Waist Away" book vividly document the physical transformation Reizer went through.

"I have written about my experience because I believe there are plenty of people living in the United States who will be able to benefit from my story. I know there are individuals out there who want to lose weight, who want to be more physically active and who want to have more energy than they currently possess. I believe I can help these people," stated Reizer.

Dr. Reizer is a 1986 magna cum laude graduate of Sherman College of Straight Chiropractic. He has been practicing chiropractic for over 20 years and is currently an Assistant Professor of Clinical Sciences at Sherman College. He maintains a private practice in Landrum, South Carolina.

"Waist Away" (ISBN 978-1-4357-0930-0) will eventually become available for purchase from most online book distributors nationwide. The text is currently available for purchase in E-Book or soft cover formats at the web address http://www.waistawaybook.com.

About The Waist Away Program:

The Waist Away Program is based on the book written and published by Dr. John Reizer. The Waist Away book details how the author lost 70 pounds by constructing his own ultra healthy diet and exercise program in 2007. For additional details please contact the author at 864-494-0121.

###

Contact: Dr. John Reizer
Phone: 864-494-0121
Email: jreizer@sherman.edu

PRESS RELEASE - FOR IMMEDIATE RELEASE:

Chiropractor Opens New Office!

Landrum, SC – Dr. John Reizer, a local chiropractor has opened a new office at 1518 East Rutherford Street. Dr. Reizer is a 1986 magna cum laude graduate of Sherman College of Straight Chiropractic in Spartanburg, South Carolina.

Dr. Reizer specializes in delivering conservative chiropractic care to all members of the community. His practice focuses on the analysis and correction of vertebral subluxations which are mechanical disorders that can occur within the framework of the spinal column. If left intact, these conditions can severely compromise the well being of the human body.

Dr. Reizer's office hours are on Monday, Wednesday, and Friday from 2:00 – 8:00 p.m. He is currently accepting new patients and can be reached at 864-494-0121.

###

In my opinion, a press release that is properly written is going to be a huge help in marketing your practice to members of your immediate community. Even if you are unable to get your press release picked up by the major newspapers, there are many distribution services you can submit the document to that will ensure your release is placed on a number of Internet search engines. This is very important because it will help to create awareness about your practice and professional name when people are looking for you on the web. Just about every person in today's society has some type of access to a computer linked to the Internet. Educated healthcare consumers will definitely look you up on line in an effort to check out your qualifications, and when they do you want to make sure they are able to find your marketing materials. The creation and proper submission of the press release document will help you to get your marketing materials into a position where they can be located by these web surfers. Keep in mind, the cost of creating and distributing this marketing tool ranges from a minimal fee to absolutely free.

The following press release services will be helpful to readers who are looking to create and distribute this type of a document:

www.24-7pressrelease.com
www.send2press.com
www.prnewswire.com

Building a Website for Your Office

The modern chiropractic office needs to have a professional looking website on the Internet. If your practice does not have a dedicated web page, you are missing out on a very important way to market your professional services to potential patients in your community.

A website address can provide a lot of valuable information to people who want to learn about your services. The great thing about the Internet is that it is active twenty-four hours a day. It even functions on holidays and at times during the year when you are away on an exotic vacation.

Once you have established a presence on the web, you can advertise the address on business cards, print media products, office brochures, bumper stickers, office newsletters and any other materials you regularly release to the public. It could hypothetically cost a chiropractor thousands of dollars to get this amount of information out to the public in a given community through traditional marketing channels. In addition, you can actually place many of your office forms that new patients will need to fill out right on your web page. New patients can regularly access and print your office forms directly from your website, and have the forms filled out before they walk into your office.

How to Get on the Internet

Getting on the Internet is really not difficult. Obviously, you could hire a company to design a professional looking website for you. You would provide the designer with the written content you would like posted on your site. Hiring a web designer to build your website from scratch could however, be an expensive project.

Another option is to simply build your own website and launch it on the Internet. Building your own web page is easier than most people think, and there are a number of companies that offer very user friendly website building tools to help you get your finished product *"up and running"* very cost effectively.

The first thing you will want to do is register a domain name for your web address. A domain name is identified by a www.youraddress.com. If, for example, your office name is the Reizer Chiropractic Center, you might consider registering a domain name that reads, www.reizerchiropracticcenter.com. You can also purchase a domain name ending with a .net, .org as well as some other options. I have purchased domain names from various sources depending upon the prices offered at a particular time. A very popular place for customers to purchase a domain name is at the web address www.register.com. This is a company that will allow you to register a domain name and purchase a website space at the same time. The domain name you purchase will be automatically integrated into a website template with very user friendly website building tools to help you create your own professional looking web address. You do not have to purchase products solely from this company as there are numerous companies for you to choose from. I only mention this particular company because they offer a very easy system for beginners to use, and the price to launch and maintain a web page with this particular company is only a few dollars each month.

      I estimate that a person who has absolutely no website building experience whatsoever could launch a basic web address for a chiropractic office in about two hours. Simply follow the tutorials provided at www.register.com, or a similar company offering comparable services, and you will be ready to be online in a short period of time.

Writing the Content for Your Web Page

When developing or designing a website, it is important to think about the content you would like potential patients to view. I like to think of a web page as a small book. It has a table of contents section that you can access with a computer mouse. The first page of your website, otherwise known as a *"landing page"* or the *"home page,"* is your opportunity to make a great first impression for web surfers. You should provide information about your office such as the physical address, the office phone number, as well as a picture of your office complex.

Additional pages on your website should cover content you feel is important for prospective and established patients to access. I have listed in this chapter some of the headings you might want to consider when adding additional pages to your own website. I want to remind you that when you build your website, you will do so one page at a time. You can do this process slowly. The home page can be published first and then you can add additional pages over the weeks and months to follow. I am constantly tweaking my own websites on a regular basis, adding fresh materials and sometimes deleting outdated content that is no longer applicable.

WEBSITE HEADINGS:

About The Doctor
My Office
Location & Map Finder
About Your First Visit
What is Chiropractic?
What is a Subluxation?
Children & Chiropractic
Frequently Asked Questions
Download Our Office Forms
Contact Us

The most important thing to remember is you want to always select a template design that is both eye pleasing and professional looking in its appearance. When you purchase your domain name and website package, most companies will offer you a large number of templates to choose from. They usually package their template options in various categories. Obviously, you should look for template designs specifically located in health related categories. Many templates will also have various color schemes for you to select from. You can end up with a very professional looking product that will give your new or established office instant credibility within your community. For about a hundred dollars and a monthly maintenance fee of approximately $8.00, you can have a presence on the web that will advertise and market your professional services around the clock.

Performing Health Talks

The health talk (lay—lecture) is a very important part of the overall process of educating laypersons. A presentation such as this is usually performed shortly after new patients begin their professional care. These presentations can also be scheduled for groups, clubs, and other organizations that exist in close proximity to your marketing territory. I highly recommend that all chiropractors make an attempt to schedule health talks/seminars with as many outside organizations as possible.

I am devoting this chapter to a discussion on the various components that make the health talk a successful patient education and marketing tool. I want chiropractors to understand just how vital these lectures are to the health of their practices. I believe that doctors who are not regularly performing health talks are definitely missing out on a great opportunity to educate patients. When you have a practice filled with educated patients, it is much easier to market additional services to them. It is also easier to convince your established patients to regularly refer you new patients.

There are many ways to construct a very successful health talk. It has been my observation that quite a few chiropractors rely on modern technology to help make their presentations a better learning experience for members of the audience. Many years ago, when I was in college, students regularly used flip charts and homemade poster boards to illustrate health talk lectures. Today, computer generated presentations which make use of the latest software programs on the market have replaced the outdated posters. Regardless of the way you illustrate your talk, most patient education experts agree that an illustrated product is much more effective in getting patients to comprehend important chiropractic concepts than a product that does not make use of illustrations.

It is my standard philosophy that everything related to the patient education process should be simplified by the chiropractor. Laypersons are generally not impressed by doctors who place sophisticated terminology into lengthy group lectures. Your patients will learn chiropractic concepts much faster if the presenter of the information makes the material interesting and understandable. The actual health talk should only take approximately thirty minutes to complete and you should always remember to keep your patient education conversations brief and very much geared toward the novice.

I can remember performing weekly health talks every Tuesday evening after my regularly scheduled office hours. I did the talks right in the office, and I required all new patients to attend the events with a spouse or a friend. I also performed many health talks for outside organizations such as utility companies, police departments, school teachers, department stores, health related support groups and any other organization that wanted to learn about the logic of chiropractic. I am confident that the health talk presentations which I performed at that time were very helpful to my cause of building a practice.

The Introduction

The introduction to your talk should be very energetic and it should immediately grab your audience's attention. An introduction also sets the stage for the rest of your presentation. It allows you to explain to listeners, in advance, what topics you will be covering and what you, their doctor, would like for them to take away from the health talk. Keep in mind that the introduction is also a chance for you to interject a little humor into the audience so that everyone attending can feel at ease. A group of relaxed patients or prospective patients, who feel comfortable in their immediate listening environment, will be able to comprehend more of what you are speaking about than those individuals who might be uptight, uncomfortable and constantly watching the clock anticipating the end of the evening.

The introduction also provides the doctor with a chance to interact with the members of the audience before the "meat" of the presentation is discussed. A doctor can size up an audience and make adjustments to the delivery style of the presentation based on the number of people in attendance and their apparent level of interest in the talk.

Writing the introduction to your health talk can be a very challenging proposition. Many chiropractors will write their introductions before attempting to create the rest of their lecture materials. By writing an introduction first, some people find it easier to create the remaining content within their presentation. Other practitioners will choose to write the main body of their talk first, and then go back to work on the introduction. In either scenario it is important that the introduction be informative, humorous, attention grabbing and successful.

Innate Intelligence

It is critical that you begin the health talk with a brief discussion about the concept of "innate intelligence." People need to understand that there is an inherent intelligence that resides within all living organisms and that this inner wisdom strives to continuously maintain order and health at all times. Every living thing has a special ability to constantly adapt to changing environmental conditions, and this is what allows life on our planet to survive. If organisms were unable to adequately adapt to changing conditions, they would die off and life as we know it would cease to exist.

A great way to begin a discussion about innate intelligence is to point out some of the many obvious examples which clearly demonstrate how living things adapt to their ever changing environments. Show your audience how people and other life forms are able to swiftly adapt to the various conditions and stresses which they regularly come into contact with.

In my talks, I often explained how the texture of human skin would change on a person's hand when an individual used a rake or a shovel for a prolonged period of time. The formation of a callus on a person's hand in response to increased pressure from a gardening tool demonstrates an inherent ability of the body to adapt to regularly occurring physical stress.

Another good example that very clearly demonstrates physiological adaptation within humans and other animals is the presence of fever during systemic infections. Fever is obviously an attempt by the body to combat infections that are challenging the integrity of an organism's well being. Many laypersons view fever as something that is quite detrimental to their own physiology. Very often, laypersons have been fed misinformation about how human physiology operates. People are constantly being exposed to media products that endorse the pharmaceutical industry's agenda of eliminating fever, and other beneficial symptoms, through the consumption of various over-the-counter medications. Many people in modern society have the distorted perception that fever is a harmful condition, and it should always be neutralized. The health talk provides the chiropractor with an opportunity to alter some of the misconceptions that are currently held by many people residing within the lay community.

The Nervous System

The next part of the health talk should include a very simple description of the human nervous system. We do not want to create an advanced anatomy lesson for members of the audience. Keep this part of the talk very short and to the point. It is also important to have great illustrations that accompany your presentation.

There are a good number of common items that can be utilized to create analogies which would help patients understand how the nervous system functions. A telephone cable, a satellite feed, television wires, radio signals, a water hose, a cell phone, a microphone, a loud speaker and probably hundreds of other examples can be used by a chiropractor to explain how the nervous system transmits signals to various parts of the body.

My favorite analogy for describing how the nervous system works is a story that tells how a conductor and his orchestra communicate. I begin by explaining how the orchestra is made up of different musical instruments. I tell laypersons that the instruments symbolize the different organs in a human being. The conductor represents the human brain, and he coordinates proper timing and cadence within the entire orchestra.

An orchestra is capable of producing beautiful music, and when all of the musicians are performing together in a concert setting, it can be one of the most wonderful events you could ever hope to experience. In an orchestra, the conductor plays an integral role in the quality of the music that is produced. If the conductor, suddenly and without warning, is disconnected from the musicians, it would not take very long for the quality of the music being played to decline. Within a short period of time the entire orchestra would probably sound awful.

This analogy provides the chiropractor with an easy way to introduce to practice members the concept of nerve interference. Most people can relate to an orchestra and its conductor. Laypersons will immediately realize that the only way the orchestra will regain its original polished sound is if the conductor is able to re-establish a direct connection with his musicians. In the case of a living person, the conductor is obviously the human brain and the song which is being played is known as health.

The use of analogies within your health talk will greatly improve a patient's ability to comprehend the information you regularly discuss. The more analogies you can come up with, the better your talk will become.

Vertebral Subluxation

The vertebral subluxation is the next topic which should be covered in the health talk. The audience has already been given an explanation about the nervous system as well as a brief introduction to the concept of nerve interference. It is now a good time to explain how a vertebral subluxation can cause a specific type of interference to a person's nervous system.

Laypersons need to understand that the damage vertebral subluxations can cause goes far beyond a simple disruption of nerve impulses between the brain and its organs. Subluxations of the spine can interfere with an individual's ability to express his or her overall health. Some chiropractors will take this theme a step further in making the claim that subluxations interfere with a human being's total expression of life.

It is vitally important that laypersons do not minimize, in their own minds, the detrimental effects of a subluxation. Many patients believe that a pinched nerve is a minor thing and not really something to get overly concerned about. Chiropractors perform a major disservice for their patients when they fail to explain that vertebral subluxations can cause very serious health problems. It should also be pointed out to the audience that subluxations always, and without exception, prevent people from expressing their full genetic potential.

It is not very likely that we will see subluxations being advertised and promoted as health risks through mainstream media products in the immediate future. Because of this fact, the chiropractor must really do a top notch job when describing a subluxation and the danger it naturally presents to the community at large. Always use a plastic model spine when discussing the subject of subluxation. Using a model gives the patient a very clear picture of what you are talking about, and you definitely want the patient to have a crisp understanding about this concept.

The three major causes of vertebral subluxations *(physical, chemical and emotional stresses)* should also be discussed. The chiropractor should give solid examples of each type of stress so that laypersons can become cognizant of the fact that most people in modern society are constantly exposed to many of these stresses on a regular basis.

The Chiropractor

The role of the chiropractor, as a professional who is specifically educated to locate, analyze and correct vertebral subluxations, should be discussed next. Laypersons and practice members should be made to understand that a chiropractor uses a number of techniques to analyze and maintain the integrity of the spinal column's alignment. A brief introduction and demonstration of the techniques a practitioner plans to use during patient care should also be offered by the presenter.

At this point in the talk, the audience should be clued in about the importance of chiropractic care for all family members. Once again I must remind readers that it is the general perception of most Americans that chiropractic is a limited therapy for musculoskeletal conditions that cause neck and back pain. The lay public believes that a chiropractor should only be consulted when people experience musculoskeletal conditions, and traditional allopathic treatments have been unsuccessful in resolving such problems.

The job of the subluxation – centered chiropractor is to make sure that every patient clearly understands the sole objective of our profession. This is a monumental task that will require the chiropractor to continuously educate patients on a regular basis. It is quite unrealistic for practitioners to expect laypersons to fully grasp "out of the box" chiropractic concepts after attending only one properly executed health talk. The chiropractor must realize that mainstream media products will always influence established chiropractic patients to view allopathic objectives as both logical and beneficial options when facing health crises. The same media products will also discourage prospective patients from seeking the professional services of a chiropractor.

Questions and Answers

At the very end of the talk, the presenter should provide the members of the audience with an opportunity to ask questions. The questions should be limited to clarifying information that was covered during the lecture. Keep answers to questions consistent with the information presented in the body of the talk so that there will not be any confusion created for other people who have successfully comprehended the information that was presented.

Write Newspaper Articles

An extremely cost effective way to market your practice is to create a well written series of newspaper articles. When a doctor writes an article that is published in a local or regional newspaper, it immediately gives the practitioner a lot of credibility in the eyes of healthcare consumers. People are more likely to read an informative news article on a health related topic than an advertisement about your office. The general public will, for the most part, ignore advertisements but pay a great deal of attention to a news story. The average person has been conditioned by constant media programming to crave news related events. Most of these cravings are centered on negative story angles that are regularly being reported. Keep this bit of information in mind when you prepare to write a headline for your article.

Once you understand the collective psyche of the population base around you, it is much easier to formulate a proper marketing strategy for your business. The suggestion I will offer to my readers is to write and publish as many articles about chiropractic as possible. Most editors of newspapers will welcome submissions from freelance writers as long as the materials being submitted are well prepared and professional in their appearance. With a little persistence, a chiropractor can get his or her stories published in a newspaper on a somewhat regular basis.

Become the Authority in Your Town

One way of establishing yourself as a well known chiropractor in your community and as an authority within your profession is to get your articles published as frequently as possible. The key to getting published in a newspaper is to develop a relationship with the editor of a particular publication you are interested in working with. I like to use the direct approach when working with editors. In most situations I will simply pick up the telephone and call a specific editor in order to conduct a meeting over the phone. Be sure to be brief and very well organized when presenting your idea to an editor because editors are extremely busy people. A good idea is to always explain to the person you are speaking with that your goal is to write a short series of articles about your professional trade. I personally let the individual know some information about my background and qualifications along with a brief outline of the type of content I am planning to write about. In addition, it is important to let the editor know the stories you will be writing about will appeal to a large number of the publication's readers. You explain to the editor that your submissions will focus on health related issues currently challenging many Americans. Once you form a professional relationship with an editor, you will have secured your foot in the publishing door.

Five Steps to Writing Chiropractic Articles:

The next item of business is to actually write your articles and to make them as professional and informative as you promised. Writing a news article is really not very difficult. There are five basic steps you should follow when preparing your story:

1. Determine the nature or purpose of your story
2. Take some time to perform research about your topic
3. Provide some "quotes" if applicable
4. Find a quiet location and write your article
5. Proofread your work!

A few years ago I decided to write an article about the subject of children carrying heavy backpacks to school. This storyline became the purpose of my article. I was genuinely concerned at the time about the number of heavy textbooks that were being placed inside these contraptions, as well as the fact that many children (my patients) were wearing these back packs everyday to school. I proceeded to interview some of my patients who had young school children and confirmed what I had originally hypothesized. The kids in my community, and probably across most of America were regularly lugging around these overstuffed backpacks.

I took a 30 minute lunch break the next day and proceeded to write my article. I have included the story below for your inspection. This particular article was published in a local community newspaper in the town where I practice chiropractic. The article was originally published in a book I wrote titled, *"Teaching Your Patients Chiropractic" ISBN 1-58961-487-9*. By the way, this is an extremely helpful book to have around if you want access to a year's supply of ready to publish chiropractic news articles.

Back Packs – Are They Safe?

Every September, young children return to school with cumbersome looking backpacks strapped over their shoulders. Many children overstuff these backpacks to such an extent that it causes a tremendous amount of physical stress to their spines.

As a practicing chiropractor in our community, I thought that it would be a good idea to remind parents to monitor the number of text books and school supplies that their children were placing inside backpacks.

The spinal column is the framework that supports the human body. It serves as an attachment point for the ribcage, muscles, and other soft tissues that are essential to a healthy human being. The spinal column is also important because it surrounds and protects the nervous system. The nervous system is responsible for transmitting important messages to various parts of the body.

Chiropractors are doctors who specialize in maintaining the integrity of the spinal column's alignment. Proper spinal alignment helps to ensure a more efficient functioning nervous system which in turn promotes better body physiology. On the other hand, inadequate spinal alignment can cause portions of the nervous system to become interfered with which can cause a multitude of physiological problems later in a person's life.

A backpack that is too heavy can injure soft tissue structures in the back which can then weaken the entire spinal column. Once the spine is compromised, it is only a matter of time before additional health problems begin to surface. Parents need to be aware of what their children are carrying around on their backs, and they should also be aware of the chiropractic profession's recommendation that a monthly chiropractic examination should be performed on every child to make sure that dangerous misalignments are not present.

Spinal misalignments, also called vertebral subluxations, are usually painless because most of the nerves that traverse between the spinal bones are not responsible for transmitting pain sensations. The nerves that enter and exit between the spinal bones transmit messages of health to the different organs and cells in the human body. If one of these nerves was to malfunction, a person would probably not be able to detect that anything was wrong. Nerve dysfunction to organs and cells inside your body will cause systemic problems to body physiology, and many of these problems will cause no observable symptoms. These serious conditions take many years to develop, and in many instances the damage caused from vertebral subluxations is permanent.

It is my personal recommendation that parents take action immediately by making an appointment for their children to see a qualified chiropractor. This is good advice that will help to keep your children functioning in a healthy manner.

Dr. John Reizer is a 1986 magna cum laude graduate of Sherman College of Straight Chiropractic. He is also the bestselling author of four books that deal with the subject of chiropractic. Dr. Reizer is an Assistant Professor of Clinical Sciences at Sherman College of Straight Chiropractic. He maintains a private practice at 1518 E. Rutherford Street in Landrum, SC. and can be reached at 864-494-0121.

At the end of my articles I always include a short paragraph which includes my marketing information. This is a highly effective way to attract new patients into your office setting. Get motivated and start writing your own stories today!

Write a Book about Your Trade

The accomplishments of writing and publishing newspaper articles will no doubt help you to effectively market your chiropractic business. As I wrote in the previous chapter, this is a marketing strategy that will immediately boost your credibility within the local community. There is however, an even better marketing concept *(writing a book)* you can use to launch your practice on the road to success. Because it is such an effective way to market any business, it is absolutely puzzling to me why more people do not take advantage of this tool. I believe many doctors probably overlook this marketing option altogether or they might be intimidated by the amount of time and work required to bring such a campaign to fruition.

Writing a book about your trade will create the perception within your local community that you are the definitive authority to speak with regarding a particular subject. It is, in my opinion, a super marketing strategy any business owner can utilize to expand a new or existing business. It can also provide additional income for the business owner while simultaneously allowing the author to make a very positive impact on the lives of many readers.

How to Write a Book

The actual process of writing a book is not as difficult as most people assume. There is a formula successful authors follow when writing a manuscript and it is advisable for anyone interested in taking on such a project to become familiar with that formula. To begin, authors should write about subjects they are familiar with. Since my readers are professionals and licensed experts within a professional trade, they will naturally be writing about a subject *(chiropractic)* they are all very familiar with.

I have personally published many books in my life and four of them have become bestsellers within the category of chiropractic. Each book I have authored represents something I created from scratch and something I can be proud of for the rest of my life. In a strange kind of way the books I have written are like my children. I have an emotional attachment to all of them because I have a vested interest in their collective well being. I want to see them grow up and become successful. Hopefully, they will reward me kindly with a tremendous amount of satisfaction *(royalties)* for many years to come. In addition, they should provide for doctors and students of chiropractic valuable information long after my professional career is over.

The initial step you should take when writing a book is to outline your manuscript. You need to divide your project into a number of workable sections/chapters. I usually divide my manuscripts into about 10 different sections when I begin this process. Once you have your sections in place, you should write about the various topics you want to cover in each section. The various sections are analogous to individual articles and eventually as the writing process unfolds, you will gradually string together the individual sections which will ultimately transform your work into a full length manuscript.

Publishing Your Book

Most authors become very frustrated after writing their books because they find it nearly impossible to locate a traditional publisher who will even take the time to review their work. The publishing industry is not very kind to new writers and when you try to submit your manuscript to most traditional publishers, they will usually not respond to your submission package. Most traditional publishers require authors to work with professional agents and they will not consider for publication an unsolicited manuscript.

I have taken the time during my writing career to research the various steps considered necessary in order to submit a manuscript to a traditional publisher. I have learned how to write a proper book proposal as well as how to prepare a professional query letter that the acquisition editors are expecting. I have written a good number of sample chapters, manuscript outlines and cover letters to various editors and agents in an effort to attract a serious offer from a traditional publisher. Most recently, I finally became successful in landing a publishing contract from such a company. At first, I was very excited about the chance to sign a contract with a traditional publisher because I had finally broken down a previously closed door. However, after carefully considering the offer presented to me, I decided against signing the contract. The publishing offer I was being asked to sign would have prevented me from having any creative input whatsoever regarding my book. The publisher would have been granted the legal right to modify large sections of my book or even prevent the book from coming out on the market place for up to two years. Additionally, the publisher had the final say and the exclusive right to prevent the book from ever being published if the company felt the market conditions had changed and no longer supported the release of such a product. The final item which convinced me to walk away from the traditional publishing contract lying on my kitchen table was the part of the agreement that stated if I signed the document; the publisher would have the right of first refusal on the next book I authored. This was so upsetting to me that I just decided to tear up the publishing agreement. I was completely disgusted with traditional publishing at that point in time, so I decided to proceed as I had done so many times in the past – I secured the services of a quality self-publisher.

Self-publishing is a wonderful tool in itself as it affords serious writers a great opportunity to get their manuscripts published, and more importantly to get their books in the hands of many readers across the nation. There are loads of self-publishers out there and they can produce a very professional product. Self-published books can be distributed successfully across the entire country and around the world. Self-publishers also utilize a newer technology that many traditional publishers have avoided. This technology is known as *"print on demand"* publishing. *"Print on demand"* publishing allows publishers to indefinitely maintain a specific book in a digital electronic file. This prevents the publisher from having to store a large number of copies in a warehouse where they might collect dust and never be sold. With *"print on demand"* technology, the books are printed, bound and shipped to the buyer within hours after they are ordered. If a consumer orders one copy or 10,000 copies of a book, it does not change how the *"print on demand"* technology operates. The ordered books are instantly processed and shipped. The money is always paid in advance by the consumer. The fees are either collected at a physical bookstore location or electronically over the Internet. With *"print on demand"* technology, the various costs associated with printing, binding, shipping, and royalties are completely accounted for long before the customer ever receives the actual copy of the book.

What this means for readers is that you can now write and publish your own books and sell them in the identical marketplace traditional publishers sell their products. Many traditional publishers cast an ugly frown in the direction of the self-publishing industry. They are quick to point out that many self-published books are substandard products. I totally disagree with this prejudiced assessment of self-publishing by the traditional publishing industry. It is almost laughable that traditional publishers will routinely criticize authors who utilize a self-publishing vehicle in order to break into a very unforgiving industry, yet they will routinely refuse to accept, for the most part, the manuscript submissions from previously unpublished authors who do not utilize professional agents. What are all of these talented and very frustrated authors, who would otherwise not have a voice, going to do? Why should these authors refuse to utilize the various services that a self-publishing company can offer? Previously unpublished authors can now have a legitimate spot within the book publishing industry. In addition, self-publishing companies pay very handsome royalties to their authors. A traditional publisher might only pay royalties in the range of 6% -8% while self-publishers can routinely pay higher royalties ranging anywhere from 45% - 99%.

In summary, let me point out the undisputable fact that writing a book about your professional trade is a tremendous opportunity for any chiropractor to market his or her practice in a unique way. I recommend you carefully explore this marketing option closely and check out some of the excellent companies that are available to help you realize your book publishing dreams. I currently utilize, and recommend with confidence, lulu.com and Amazon.com as fine self-publishing companies.

Brochures, Posters & Models

Brochures, posters, and models are all very important marketing tools you will want to utilize within a chiropractic practice. All of these items can be very effective if they are used properly. Just hanging a rack of brochures up on the wall, or hanging a poster in your office is not going to get the job done. That is not using these tools properly. That is only displaying the tools. If you want these items to be effective in your patient education program, you must learn how to use them.

Let me begin by writing about brochures. What types of brochures should you include inside of your office? How many of them are necessary for you to place in the office? You should stock the types of brochures that best represent the type of practice you have chosen to operate. It is important for you to select brochure titles that are congruent with the practice type you have subscribed to. If you have decided to specialize in the area of pediatrics, you will want to have brochures that focus on chiropractic for kids. A personal injury practice will most likely have brochures that focus on automobile accidents or whiplash injuries. The same holds true for geriatric practices and an office set up to accommodate a family wellness clientele. There are many companies that offer a large selection of brochure titles. Brochures are generally inexpensive and most companies will send you free samples so you can read through their content before you decide to purchase any products. I recommend you shop around, get some samples and only choose titles that fit within the genre of your office mission. There is no limit to the number you can have. You can even rotate your titles every month or two in order to keep the information fresh.

Once you have selected your brochure titles, you have to know how to utilize them. Like I stated earlier, there is a difference between displaying and effectively using brochures. Initially, you must make sure you are familiar with the content of any brochure you place in your office. A brochure stands a much better chance of being read if you, the doctor, personally hand out the publication to your patient. The chances of being read are even greater if you open up the brochure, point to or circle a certain section, and tell the patient you would like him or her to pay particular attention to a specific topic. When your patient returns for the next visit, you will have another opportunity to educate that person by asking the patient if you can answer any questions he or she may have about the publication. This is much more effective than just sending a patient home with eight or nine different brochures. Always make the educational process memorable.

While I am on the subject of brochures, I would like to also point out that it is a very good idea to have a publication featuring your own office. You can make this yourself on almost any desktop publishing software package and have the brochures printed at an office supply store for a minimal investment. These make great handouts for new or potential patients at health screenings.

The posters you purchase for your office should also be selected based on the practice type you have chosen to specialize in. They should be visible in the waiting room, exam rooms, x-ray rooms and anywhere else patients will spend time in your office. Use them as a way to start a chiropractic conversation. A poster demonstrating the phases of subluxation degeneration comes in very handy during your report of findings presentation. Use it to compare the patient's radiographs with one of the phases of degeneration. This becomes a very powerful tool as well as a very powerful motivator when a patient sees his or her problem did not just happen overnight.

Use a poster to illustrate posture in order to point out some of the findings associated with a patient's exam or to point out what to look for in a spouse or a child. The educational possibilities are absolutely endless as long as you use the posters and not just display them.

Models are another very useful marketing tool. No office should ever be without a model spine. This should be used in your five minute new patient orientation, your report of findings, your health talk, or any other time you feel a patient needs a more thorough, visual explanation of what you are discussing. There is no better tool on the market to show what a vertebral subluxation looks like and how very little movement it takes to impinge a nerve. You should also use your model spine to show a patient how many subluxations you have detected and where and how you will be making adjustments to correct the problems.

Learn How to Identify Prospective Patients

There is a definite methodology to identifying prospective patients for your professional practice. This subject is an extremely important part of the overall strategy to create more cost effective marketing strategies for your chiropractic business.

We chiropractors, for the most part, have very limited funds when it comes to marketing and advertising. It is therefore very important we work smart and make the most out of the limited resources that are at our disposal. By selecting only the best potential candidates to market our professional services to, we will have a much better chance of having overall success in our total marketing efforts as well as our abilities to create a well educated chiropractic healthcare consumer.

It is pointless to waste time, energy and finances on marketing campaigns positioned in the direction of healthcare consumers who do not want to purchase what you have to sell. I often dedicate a lecture to my college students on this very subject and explain in some detail to them why most marketing strategies are not cost effective and really a bad idea.

Imagine for a moment you are trying to sell exterior vinyl siding to homeowners across America. You have decided to market your product by blindly calling five hundred new prospects every day on the telephone. Let me explain to you why this is a bad way to market your vinyl siding. First of all, a certain percentage of the prospects you plan to call will not even own a home. Some of these people might be renters, or they might not be the decision maker at the residence you are calling. Secondly, an additional percentage of the prospects you plan to call will own a new home and will not be in need of exterior vinyl siding. Because you decided to pitch your product in this manner, you have automatically wasted time and energy speaking to individuals not interested in buying what you have to offer. It is quite predictable that your marketing results will most likely be very poor at best.

Now, I want you to imagine another scenario where you are pitching the same vinyl siding product over the telephone. You also have the same goal of calling five hundred prospects every day; however this time the list of potential customers you are planning to contact will be stacked in your favor. Every person you speak with this time will want the very product you are trying to sell. Do you think your results might be a lot better considering every potential customer you are going to call will be in the market for vinyl siding? Obviously the answer is yes. The results of your marketing campaign are going to be drastically improved when you market your product or service directly to individuals that are already looking for what you have to offer. This is the scenario you want to replicate when you market your professional service to prospective patients. You want to create a system that allows you to market chiropractic care to only those people who are looking to buy your professional healthcare service.

Categorize Your Prospects

The first item of business you will want to take care of within your practice is to separate all potential prospects and place them into three defined categories:

1. Prospects who want your service
2. Prospects who are interested in your service
3. People who do not want your service

The second item of business is to eliminate the third category of people. Why would you want to waste money marketing to people who have no intention of doing business with you? Do not bother trying to educate people who fall into this category. Your efforts, your money and your creative talents need to be focused only on the first two categories of prospects.

The third item of business is to construct a very efficient database of good potential prospects made up from people in the first two categories. Once again, at the expense of sounding redundant, let me reiterate the point that these are the only people you should spend time, energy and money marketing your services to.

Building a Database

Building a database of prospective patients is not very hard. You will need to purchase (if you do not already have one) a personal or business computer that can create and keep track of a list of names.

One place prospective patients can come from is through leads from already existing marketing programs which you have implemented in your practice. Since many of these leads are probably of high quality, it is likely these individuals will be converted to actual patients in your office. The names of these prospective patients should therefore be added to your database.

Another good source of prospective patients that should be added to your database is the names of any persons who have previously contacted you for information about your professional services. Whenever a person calls your office, it is extremely important to write down his or her name, address, and phone number. Any individual who calls and requests information about your professional service is a good potential prospect. In this situation you already know the person has a genuine interest in what you have to offer. This individual is a good candidate to market your service to and he or she should be placed into the database of names you are creating.

Perhaps the best way to fill your database with the names of good prospects is through a *lead generation system*. This is a system of marketing that has been used with great success for a number of years. Lead generation campaigns are widely used in the insurance and real estate industries. There are many companies that specialize in this type of marketing, and their entire area of focus is centered on providing clients with the names of prospective customers who are eager to purchase certain products or services. I am quite sure my readers are familiar with companies that sell mailing lists to various clients. Mailing lists are usually made up of the names of people who have requested or purchased certain products and services in the past. Clients will purchase mailing lists because they want to market their own products to these consumers. The mailing list industry is a type of lead generation program.

Lead generation systems can work with any product or service in just about any imaginable industry. The concept is based on a scientific principle that has been proven time and time again. I think the reason some people refer to it as a science is because of the high rate of success a system such as this yields, and also the fact that the results are regularly reproducible.

The way that this process works is to simply place a small advertisement in a newspaper or magazine that gives a brief description of a product or service somewhat appealing to certain segments of the population. Within the advertisement, a phone number or a website address is provided so a prospective customer can get additional information about a said product. When the prospective customer calls for additional information, his or her name is thrown into a database and the information requested is immediately sent to the prospect in the form of a free publication, DVD, or pamphlet. From that point forward the prospect is kept on a database (mailing list) and the company will spend money in the future, marketing their products or services to the individual and other people on the database. The chances are extremely good that the people in the database will purchase the products and services the company is selling. There is no wasted marketing with this type of a system as all efforts to sell products and services are projected only in the direction of people who want to purchase what the company has to sell.

In addition, there is only minimal cost incurred when placing advertisements in media products because the sizes of the advertisements are very small. Keep in mind the goal of a lead generation system is to create a database of good prospects for a company to market to, and also to educate the various consumers about products and services through the regular mailing of publications, DVD's and pamphlets. Publications and pamphlets are much more cost effective to produce than large newspaper ads randomly targeted to many thousands of people who couldn't care less about many of the items a particular company might be selling.

The construction of a database through the utilization of the three methods discussed in this chapter is a great way to market chiropractic services to a highly desirable group of healthcare consumers.

I have written a sample advertisement and publication explaining about the benefits of subluxation – centered chiropractic services. I have placed the sample materials in this chapter so my readers can observe how the system can work for a practicing chiropractor. Both the advertisement and publication have actually been used repeatedly in my private practice and they have yielded solid prospects that eventually lead to the generation of new chiropractic patients.

Persons who are interested in using the sample materials for their own private practice may do so free of charge.

Sample Advertisement and Publication

> # Doctor Explains
> # How to Improve Health Naturally!
>
> *Anywhere, USA*—*Previously suppressed information about healthcare has just been published by a doctor within the community. The published information explains how to improve health naturally, and without dangerous drugs. Interested persons should call the phone number listed below to have a copy of this published information sent directly to them. There is no charge for the published information and callers will not be required to buy anything. Call* **123-456-7890** *and listen to the recorded message.*
>
> Copyright © January 2005 Dr. John L. Reizer

How to Improve Health Naturally

> Copyright © January 2005
> By Dr. John L. Reizer
> All Rights Reserved!

WARNING! – This publication contains suppressed information. What you are about to read may actually change the way you currently think. Most people in the world have probably never been made aware of the information that I am about to reveal. I want you to have an open mind when reading this material and I need to warn you ahead of time that some of the subject matter will absolutely shock you! Regardless of the amount of shock this publication creates for various individuals, it is important that Americans learn about its contents so that they will be better informed when making decisions about healthcare.

Healthcare is big business and it generates billions of dollars in profits on an annual basis. If you were only permitted to learn one essential item about running a successful business, you would want to know that it is the goal of every company to constantly increase its profits while trying to find new and creative ways to expand existing business. In a nutshell, you want more customers who need or utilize your products and services. Most people believe that the healthcare industry (pharmaceutical industry) is in the business of getting sick people well. It is this be**lie**f that allows the overall health of our population to continuously decline a little more each year.

As the years pass it seems as though more terrifying diseases are arriving on the scene. ***Autoimmune disorders, cancer, AIDS, diabetes, cardiovascular problems, viruses,*** and many other serious health conditions continue to make their way into our lives. On the surface it is made to look like the pharmaceutical companies are burning the oil day and night in an attempt to find a cure for these deadly diseases. Can you picture all of the scientists in a very sophisticated laboratory setting, donned in white gowns peering down into rows of microscopes? It is the hope of the average person that one of these scientists will produce a cure for *cancer* or for one of the other previously mentioned plagues currently terrorizing humanity. Don't hold your breath! It's not going to happen in your lifetime or even your children's lifetime for that matter.

Do you know how much money is made by pharmaceutical companies each year for the treatment of *cancer*? What about for the treatment of ***AIDS, diabetes, heart disease, hypertension, influenza, lupus, the common cold, headaches, depression, or rheumatoid arthritis?*** The answer is billions of dollars. That's right – billions of dollars are earned every year by multinational pharmaceutical companies that have patents on various drugs that are used to treat symptoms associated with these deadly diseases.

Pharmaceutical companies depend on these diseases to make large profits every year. It wouldn't be very smart for a pharmaceutical company to conduct research that would lead to a cure for a specific disease. Why would a company want to destroy a cash cow?

The healthcare industry is in the business of managing symptoms and conditions of sickness. There is not much money to be made by producing cures, but quite a lot of money is collected in the management of various diseases. The sicker people get the more drugs they will require and the more profits to be made by the pharmaceutical companies. This is a vicious cycle and it is quite a convenient scenario for an industry that is determined to expand its market annually.

In the United States there have been attempts by certain individuals, groups, and even some alternative healthcare professions to try and stop this abuse. These attempts have been met with much resistance from powerful healthcare unions that receive unlimited funds from pharmaceutical companies. Many people have had their careers and families ruined because they attempted to disclose this information to the general public. Professions have been absorbed and redesigned with newer objectives that were congruent with the pharmaceutical industry's way of thinking. **You have to understand that big money is at stake here.**

One alternative healthcare profession has managed to survive for many years. It has a simple philosophy and a professional objective that makes so much sense that it infuriates the allopathic (traditional medical) community. This healthcare philosophy has been attacked by traditional medicine for many years. **In 1987 Federal Judge Susan Getzendanner of the United States District Court found the American Medical Association, the American College of Radiologists, the American College of Surgeons, as well as many other medical organizations guilty of conspiring to destroy this profession.** This is not a Hollywood movie script. This really happened and the guilty parties only received a slap on the wrist.

This alternative healthcare profession has a single objective which is to remove a certain type of interference from the body that causes human physiology and chemistry not to work properly. By removing this type of interference from the body, the physiology within a human being operates more efficiently and many conditions of sickness are then resolved naturally via the body's own immune system. **This is a powerful concept and information such as this could really help humanity. Unfortunately, this concept doesn't promote the sale of pharmaceutical products so you will never see it promoted in any form of national or international media.**

So what is the name of this mystery profession and where did it come from? This profession has been around for thousands of years. Ancient Egyptians used this healing art and so did the Chinese and the Greek cultures. Many secret societies passed this knowledge on to other civilizations during the course of many thousands of years. In the late 1800's it was introduced to the modern world and was given a new name – **CHIROPRACTIC.**

Chiropractic has been under attack for many years and when one fully understands the logic behind this profession's objective, it is easy to see why the multi-billion dollar drug industry would not want it around.

Chiropractic and its practitioners represent a major threat to the traditional healthcare professions. The strong medically backed unions have made it a top priority throughout the years to try and silence this lone voice of common sense in an otherwise insane industry.

The beauty of chiropractic is that it is so simple to understand that even a young child could comprehend how it works with the controlling laws of nature.

HERE'S HOW IT WORKS!

The human brain sends and receives messages to and from all parts of the body. It is essential that these messages arrive at specific pre-determined locations inside the body at certain times of the day in order for health to be maintained in a human being. These messages travel inside the spinal cord and spinal nerves. This system is like a giant telephone communication network. The spinal cord and spinal nerves are protected by the spinal bones and the brain is protected by the skull. Spinal bones (vertebrae) are moveable structures, and they allow us a great deal of flexibility when we move around. Because the spinal bones sit on top of one another, they form a long canal of bones where the spinal cord runs through. The spinal nerves that exit off of the spinal cord pass between openings that are made on the sides of the spinal bones. Sometimes spinal bones become misaligned from each other and this causes them to place a slight amount of pressure on the spinal nerves. When this happens, the messages that are being transmitted through the nervous system become garbled and this causes problems to occur in the body's physiology.

Chiropractors will nudge the spinal bones back into their proper anatomical positions by making gentle manual (by hand) adjustments. This is not done to treat specific conditions of sickness but rather to correct the misaligned (subluxated) spinal bones. **The spinal adjustments help to remove nerve interference, and this allows health to be restored in the body naturally.** Many conditions of sickness are then reversed by the body's own inborn recuperative abilities.

I invite you to explore this amazing preventive healthcare profession further by making an appointment at my office. It is a health investment that will pay you dividends for many years to come.

SPECIAL OFFER!

Because you took the time to read this publication *I am going to waive the usual $XX.00 initial visit and consultation fee. (X-rays and treatment if necessary are not included in this offer.) This will allow you to visit my office, receive a complete chiropractic examination and consultation by a professional doctor all at no charge to you.* There will be no obligation on your part to become a patient at my practice. I urge you however, to make an appointment immediately so that you can learn about a more intelligent way to promote general health and well being throughout your own body. I look forward to seeing you.

***END OF SAMPLE PUBLICATION ***

By following the simple advice I have written, a chiropractor can drastically reduce his or her external marketing expenses. Unfortunately, most chiropractors will not follow the recommendations I have outlined and they will spend excessive amounts of advertising dollars on external marketing campaigns that target the people in category number three which I wrote about earlier in this chapter. Remember, the third category represented the people who do not want to purchase your professional service.

I disagree with many advertising experts who profess about the importance of having a broad scope external marketing program that targets every person who is breathing. This strategy is not helpful in bringing new patients into the chiropractic office setting. I want chiropractors to understand that the most efficient and effective way to launch a successful external marketing program is to **identify prospective patients, place them into a database and then regularly utilize a direct mailing program that targets only those prospects within your database**. This strategy is going to give you the best results for your advertising dollar.

I am not saying other forms of external marketing should never be attempted by chiropractors. I believe in the concept that a general presence should be maintained in the real *Yellow Pages* (the company responsible for maintaining your business phone line) as well as some local newspapers or similar print media products that are going to provide doctors with opportunities for professional exposure. In the case of the newspaper, readers should remember it is always helpful if you are able to contribute to a publication by authoring a weekly column or a series of articles as I mentioned earlier in this book. Remember, this will help to establish your credibility as an expert within chiropractic.

Teach a Community College Course

When I opened my first chiropractic office back in 1987, I decided to teach a community college course on chiropractic. My rationale, at the time, was to create some awareness in my town about the professional services I would be offering. I always enjoyed the process of trying to teach others about the principles of chiropractic. When I was a student in college, I often tutored fellow chiropractic students that were having a difficult time with a particular subject. The idea of teaching others fascinated me and as it turned out it also provided me with an opportunity to personally develop my communication skills that I would regularly rely upon when I became a successful practicing chiropractor and many years later as a college faculty member at Sherman College.

Initially, the thought of teaching a community college course seemed like a logical way for me to build my new practice. I had never attempted to formally teach others about chiropractic in a college classroom setting. I had performed a few health talks as a student in chiropractic college for various patients, but that was the extent of my experience with teaching a group of people.

The concept of teaching a community college course over a ten week schedule would be a new challenge for me and I have to admit I found the opportunity both scary and exciting at the same time. It was my basic nature however, to never let something new or challenging stop me from proceeding with my goals. I rationalized that I would only be nervous for the first few minutes of the first class and then the entire scene would become more comfortable for me. As it turned out, this is exactly what happened.

This opportunity presented itself after I called the local community college's administrative offices in the town where I practiced and explained to them my idea for the course. I told the director of the program that I wanted to teach laypersons the many benefits of chiropractic and I would also explore the possibilities of a career in chiropractic for the students taking the class. The director loved my idea and immediately encouraged me to develop the course for the next semester.

The name of my new course was *"Better Health through Chiropractic"* and I immediately wrote a syllabus which was basically a very long version of my new patient orientation and health talk presentation. I broke down the course into ten weekly sections and I scheduled the entire class to meet at my private practice during the middle of the semester. During that week I conducted, for the entire class, a tour of my office facilities and I offered each student a complimentary spinal screening. The course became an instant success for me and it was very popular amongst the community education students. I ended up teaching this particular course for several years and it always provided me with a fresh supply of new patients for my private practice.

Teaching a community education course about chiropractic is a great way to market a doctor's professional services to many people in a given neighborhood. It is just another way chiropractors can set themselves apart from other practitioners while creating the perception that they are the authorities within their chosen profession or trade.

This is a highly effective marketing tool for chiropractors to utilize and it will not cost a practitioner any money whatsoever to run this program. In fact, the community college will most likely end up paying the chiropractor a few hundred dollars each semester to be an instructor. Not a bad set up when one thinks about the overall picture being painted. The doctor is paid to market his or her private practice each semester and is perceived as an authority within the profession who is a caring individual and a person willing to give back time and knowledge to the general community.

Teaching a community college course about chiropractic is a very cost effective marketing tool and I recommend that my readers begin the process of developing and implementing their own courses for the next semester as soon as possible.

Create a Patient Referral Program

Every chiropractor would like to know some sure-fire marketing techniques that will bring lots of new patients into his or her private office setting. The marketing techniques that work the best are usually simple in their design and not that complicated to implement into a professional practice. One thing you will need to do is to come to terms with the fact that the chiropractic profession usually does not receive much in the way of cooperative advertising from the media or other health related fields. In other words you are not going to get a tremendous amount of help in building your practice from outside sources. If you want to build a large patient base, you are going to have to do this task on your own.

A very cost effective marketing tool is to make sure that you create an efficient patient referral program that will ensure your practice receives a constant stream of new patients on a regular basis. You will need to teach your patients the importance of referring others for professional services.

As a chiropractor, it is extremely important that you learn to become a very effective communicator. This skill will be utilized often when building your patient referral system.

You will need to teach already existing patients how to properly refer new prospects into your office. You will do this simply by teaching your practice members the importance of chiropractic care for the entire family. Let your existing patients know that chiropractic is a valuable service for all people who have a desire to be healthy. Existing patients will also need to be able to understand simple chiropractic principles and, more importantly, they must be able to convey the principles to other lay persons within the community.

Fortunately, most of the principles that laypersons will need to learn, in order to regularly refer patients into your office, are very simple concepts to understand. Make sure that you keep these concepts simple when presenting them to your patients. Resist the urge to make things more complicated than they need to be when going through your explanations with patients. It is human nature to take something that is very simple and to make it more complex. If you do this you will not have a successful referral campaign.

Teach the Five Concepts

The first concept you will need to teach to patients is how the body is always trying to maintain itself in a healthy state of existence. Give an explanation on how the body does everything in its power to keep itself healthy and how in situations where it has become compromised by sickness it will do everything possible to try and restore order.

The second concept you will need to teach to patients is how health is maintained naturally with the help of the human nervous system. Explain to your patients how the brain, spinal cord, and spinal nerves help to transmit electrical messages *(instructions for health)* to all areas of the body and that this ultimately ensures health in human beings.

The third concept you will teach to your patients is how the spinal bones protect the nervous system from detrimental external forces while simultaneously allowing humans the ability to move around with a great deal of agility.

The fourth concept you must teach to your patients is how misalignments of the spinal bones (subluxations) can interfere with the delivery and transmission of the electrical messages inside the nervous system. You must teach patients that the normal tendencies for the body to be healthy are largely dependent on these electrical messages being transmitted through the nervous system properly and without any interference.

The fifth and final concept you must teach to your patients is how a chiropractic spinal adjustment is capable of correcting a subluxation within the spinal column. You need patients to understand that when a subluxation is removed from the equation, the interference within the nervous system is eliminated and this allows the body to express itself once again in a healthy manner.

These concepts will appear quite logical to laypersons the very first time they have a chance to hear them. If they are presented properly by the chiropractor to already existing patients, it will not take very long for those patients to be able to relate the chiropractic story to other laypersons within the community. This can be a very powerful referral tool for your practice once you learn how to utilize the system properly.

Create an Incentive Plan

The next thing you must do is to create an incentive plan for your patients to go out and sell your service. Some of your patients will become motivated to generate referrals for your practice just from their understanding of these five chiropractic concepts and they will not require an incentive from you to get the job done. You should be prepared however to offer the patients in your practice some kind of an incentive to ensure the program's success. You need to understand that most people enjoy recognition for a job that has been competently performed. My suggestion is that you thank your patients on a regular basis for the referrals which they send to your office. Saying thank you to a patient that is helping you to build your practice is easy. A handshake, a post card in the mail, an email communication on the Internet, a message board featuring the patient's name and accomplishment posted in a conspicuous location within your office are very acceptable ways to thank patients. In addition to saying thank you, it wouldn't hurt to reward patients with an occasional gift certificate to a movie theatre or to a popular department store. Perhaps you might even consider issuing a t-shirt which advertises your practice to the patient who generates the most referrals within a given month. *(**Once again, check with your state's chiropractic board to see if a particular incentive reward is legal.**)*

Helpful Tools

There are a number of very good chiropractic books on the market that have been specifically written to teach laypersons important chiropractic principles. In 2002 I personally authored the book *"Chiropractic Made Simple: Working With the Controlling Laws of Nature" Wincan Publishing*. This book can be purchased from Amazon.com as well as from many other Internet book distributors around the world. I highly recommend that you have your patients read this text at some point. *"Chiropractic Made Simple"* teaches patients the importance of wellness care and it also teaches patients the importance of referring others. Many chiropractors in the United States now require their new patients to read this book before getting under care.

Keep in mind that incentive based referral programs are very well received in the chiropractic office environment. If structured properly, the existing patients within your private practice will regularly generate hundreds of new patient referrals on an annual basis. In the end, this will allow you to focus more of your attention on helping your patients.

Outside marketing procedures will probably continue to be a necessary part of your overall practice building strategies; however the pressures to bring in newer prospects via the use of external marketing campaigns will be significantly reduced once you implement this type of a program.

Market Your Service to Health Clubs

A chiropractor has to approach an external marketing campaign realistically. I firmly believe that in order to attract quality patients that are going to be serious about their healthcare needs, the practitioner must look in all the right places when commencing the marketing process. Chiropractors are famous for marketing their businesses to the wrong groups of people and eventually become very frustrated when their external marketing programs are not successful.

As I wrote in a previous chapter, too many of us devote a lot of our precious time and energy marketing to people who will never see the value of our professional services. Why market professional services to these people in the first place? Instead, we should be marketing to prospects more likely to utilize chiropractic services.

There are many people in our communities interested in visiting a chiropractor. You just have to figure out where these prospects are actually hiding in your town. The answer to the puzzle is that many good prospects are hiding in great numbers at health fitness clubs all across America. People interested in visiting chiropractors are usually quite health conscious. These prospects have a strong desire to take care of their bodies and can be found in gyms working out and keeping physically fit. They are actually fitness consumers, and they want to be healthier than the average person. If you want to find health conscious people, you have to market your services to health clubs.

Join a Health Club

The first item of business that chiropractors should take care of is to join a health fitness club. This will benefit the doctors in a couple of ways. To begin with, the chiropractors will be in close proximity to fitness consumers and regularly forming relationships with like minded people who have a strong commitment to becoming and staying healthy. Secondly, the doctors will be performing a big service for themselves by keeping their own bodies physically fit which will probably prolong both their lives and professional careers.

During the first twelve years that I practiced, I was a regular member at a fitness center in the town where I owned my business. I routinely picked up a lot of new patients just by talking with fellow members. They just needed to find out I was a chiropractor which was pretty easy for me to disclose. I wore to the fitness center a couple of T-shirts with my advertisement information printed on the front side of the shirts, and before I knew it people were coming up to me and asking advice about various conditions they had been experiencing. I always carried with me an ample supply of business cards because I never wanted to let a marketing opportunity get away from me. I was also approached by one of the club's managers and asked to perform a mini health seminar and spinal screening for the various members. Within a relatively short period of time, I was well known within the gym as an established chiropractic expert. The best part of the entire scenario was that my office was just down the road, and most of the club's members were very familiar with where I was located. It was just that simple and it gave my practice a phenomenal boost in the business category of taking on new patients.

This is absolutely a worthwhile investment of both your time and money. I can assure you, from personal experience, a number of new patients will sign up at your practice just from the act of you joining a health fitness facility. The word will definitely get out to the other members and everything else will fall into place.

Market a Weight Loss Campaign

In January, 2007 I decided to weigh myself on a bathroom scale and instantly confirmed what I had suspected for quite a lengthy period of time – I was extremely overweight! I hadn't stepped on a scale in about two years and I knew that I was out of shape, but I had no idea just how heavy and out of shape I had become.

I decided that it was finally time to view the damage and so after some moments of quiet contemplation, I convinced myself that I needed to step on that bathroom scale. As the numbers flickered to life, they gradually settled at the ridiculous weight of 245 pounds. I instantly became very depressed. Those feelings of depression were soon replaced by the feelings of anger and later by fear. I was disgusted, depressed and scared at the same time.

Up to that point in time it had been very easy for me to rationalize about being comfortable with my weight. It's quite amazing how a person can, over a period of time, continue to gain weight and for the most part be unaware of the actual accumulation of extra pounds on his or her body. In some respects it is analogous to a snow storm. You do not hear the snow flakes as they come floating down from the clouds above. The next morning when you look out your front window, you see that the storm delivered several feet of snow on the ground. You're left with a mess to clean up. The same can be said about gaining weight. The process of weight gain seems quite innocuous as it is taking place, but eventually it leaves you with a heck of a problem over time.

Looking back at my own situation, it became obvious to me that I had been living in a constant state of denial for a number of years. A blizzard had taken place inside me and I finally realized that I had become trapped in a body that was 70 pounds too heavy.

My professional background as a healthcare provider immediately sent warning signals to my educated mind. I knew that I had to weather this storm and get my problem under control fast. I remember quite vividly coming out to the living room to talk with my wife about my new found discovery. I told her with a great amount of emotion in my voice that *I was a fat slob*. She smiled and proceeded to start laughing. She and I had both known for a couple of years that I had a serious weight problem. It had struck her funny when I came out of the bathroom and declared myself fat. We both laughed for a few moments and then discussed my dilemma in a more serious manner.

Over the past couple of years my weight gain had caused me to develop a serious problem with snoring. My poor wife could not even sleep in the same room with me because my snoring kept her up the entire night. This snoring issue became the source of many heated arguments between us. On numerous occasions I can remember instructing her not to keep waking me from a deep sleep. I reasoned with her that at least one of us should be able to get some rest. On yet another occasion, I went on a business trip with my brother to Sacramento, California where we shared a hotel room. The initial morning after we slept in that hotel room my brother presented me with a tape recording that he had made of me snoring during the previous night. He commented that he never heard anyone snore as loud as me. When I listened to the tape, I could not believe my ears. I had no idea just how much my problem had progressed.

Another problem I had developed over the past couple of years was a constant lack of energy. It seemed as though I was always tired. This lack of energy was quite annoying. I wanted to be more physically active, but it seemed that a nap or sitting in front of the television was a more attractive choice for me. I was also beginning to experience episodes of shortness of breath when I would have to walk up a hill or climb a set of stairs. This, more than any other symptomatic change in my life, began to grab my attention and ultimately initiated the process of waking me up from the coma like trance I had been stuck in.

For a good portion of my life I had been in very good physical shape. In my high school years I excelled in organized sports such as baseball and football. As I mentioned in the previous chapter, during my years in college and even after I graduated from chiropractic college I remained very active, running and exercising at a fitness center several times a week. Throughout my 20's and well into my 30's I did a tremendous amount of running as well. I would often run about 20 – 30 miles a week on an indoor track. I usually maintained a weight right around 175 pounds during those years. I am approximately 5' 11 inches tall and I have always believed that I looked and felt my best at this weight.

In January, 2007 I was far away from looking and feeling good. I was also far away from my optimum weight of 175 pounds. During the past 8 years I had lived a more sedentary and stressful lifestyle than ever before. My employment as an assistant professor at a chiropractic college in those years had been quite enjoyable to me, but the position also brought a great deal of stress into my life.

The demands of academia as well as adapting to a new lifestyle that came along with the birth of my beautiful daughter in 2001 presented me with a number of stresses that I had not previously experienced. I also authored 5 books over a 4 year span of time. My focus had been centered on a word processor and not on an indoor track where I would have been dedicated to a workout program. When you regularly engage in *brain work,* you often feel like you are working hard, but in a physical sense you are hardly working. I did not get fat and out of shape in one or two weeks. It took a major commitment to living a completely sedentary lifestyle to accomplish the amount of weight gain that I had achieved.

The simple facts were that I was 70 pounds overweight, I had little or no energy, I was regularly experiencing episodes of shortness of breath when taking part in light exercise and I was very much terrified about my predicament. I really had no idea what to do to get myself out of this situation. I was scared to admit to anyone that I had a serious problem. In January, 2007 I believed that I needed the services of a trained professional in order to help me out of my living hell. I knew that if I continued with my current lifestyle that I probably would not live for very long.

    My healthcare training as a licensed doctor of chiropractic made it clear to me that I was probably facing a lifetime of weight related health disorders such as diabetes, cardiovascular problems, autoimmune challenges, and increased pressure on my skeletal system which also increased my chances of developing osteoarthritis throughout most of the bony joints in my body. I knew that there were a multitude of other potential health problems that I would quite possibly encounter if I actually lived long enough. Basically, the entire quality of my life would become substandard if I did not solve this problem. One way or another, I had to save my life, and I felt that I had to take action immediately.

More Determined Than Ever

At the age of 44 I knew I was classified as an obese person. I was writing bestselling books on the subject of chiropractic and deeply involved in the process of educating future doctors while simultaneously giving out advice to my patients in a private practice setting. I thought to myself, *why would anyone want to take healthcare advice from someone who was obese and out of shape?* I then asked myself an even more painful question. *Would I take healthcare advice from someone who looked like me?* After thinking the question over for a few seconds, the answer I came up with was – no!

I was definitely not feeling very good about myself at this point. After reviewing all of this information in my mind, I knew deep down inside that I had absolutely reached a critical point in my life and it was time to take immediate action. I was more determined than ever to carry out my plan. I could be a very disciplined and determined person if I put my mind on something. I felt for the first time in many years that I had the focus and the proper attitude to get my weight problem corrected permanently. If

I failed to correct my problem, I was very aware of the health risks that I would have to face.

My Success Story

I created a blue print that absolutely saved my life. I then proceeded to write a book about how I accomplished my goals (www.waistawaybook.com) so that I could share my success story with patients, family members and friends. I wrote about my experience because I believed there were many people living in the United States who would directly benefit from the information I had uncovered. I knew these people wanted to lose weight, wanted to be more physically active and wanted to have more energy than they currently possessed. I had miraculously changed my own life in just 7 months and I believed that many folks could replicate my results. The people who knew me personally were amazed at the physical changes I underwent in just a short period of time.

I was able to accomplish the personal goal of losing 70 pounds in 7 months without any type of arduous exercise program, expensive gym equipment, prepackaged food plans, dangerous drugs or surgical procedures. I was also able to accomplish the personal goal of eating a healthy diet of quality foods, and I never once starved or deprived myself of any valuable nutritional requirements.

As I was writing my weight loss book, ***"Waist Away: How I Lost 70 Pounds in 7 Months Without Drugs or Surgery"*** I absolutely believed it was important for me to try and help my chiropractic patients figure out a way to set and accomplish similar personal weight loss goals. People who are overweight or obese have a very hard time maintaining the integrity of their spinal alignment. I struggled taking care of overweight patients for many years, trying to manage them through a conservative program of chiropractic care.

Whenever doctors are able to educate themselves with valuable information about healthcare concepts, I feel it is important that they share the material with others. Because we carry the title of doctor, *(the Latin translation for the word doctor is teacher)* I believe we have an even bigger obligation than the average person to follow through on revealing important information about health related topics to laypersons. I know from experience that the acquisition and delivery of healthcare knowledge, through the reading and writing of books, is an essential component in keeping the members of our society at an optimal level of health. Because of this fact, I currently encourage all chiropractors to market weight loss programs within their private practices.

Sixty-six percent of Americans are overweight or obese and I know many chiropractors continue to have heavy patients coming in for care. Just from a financial perspective alone it makes a lot of sense for doctors to implement weight loss programs in their practices. There is a tremendous monetary incentive awaiting chiropractors who choose to enter this multibillion dollar arena. A weight loss campaign will, no doubt, add a lucrative stream of income to a new or existing practice. I recently added the "Waist Away Weight Loss Program" in my practice as a service for patients. The beauty of the "Waist Away" campaign is that it is easy and profitable for chiropractors to market. My patients continue to come in for subluxation correction care and they are sent home with a copy of the "Waist Away" book that I authored. All patients are assigned a plan of care that will maintain proper spinal alignment for them throughout the entire year. They are also directed to follow the advice in the book. The overweight or obese patients in any chiropractic practice will absolutely gain a lot of benefit from following my program. These patients will have better spinal alignment as well as constant support from a caring professional as they try to create positive lifestyle habits that will ultimately allow them to lose weight and then maintain the weight loss results they achieve over a lifetime.

My book explains the entire logical process which I developed and it promotes four very important principles of weight loss success that absolutely work. Keep in mind that the book also promotes the importance of regular chiropractic care in order to maintain a properly functioning nervous system which obviously leads to a healthier metabolic rate for all patients.

I invite readers to visit my weight loss website that was listed in the beginning of this chapter. My story can absolutely help your overweight patients and possibly quite a few doctors to become healthier. The protocols in my book/program do not require patients to purchase any supplements. The program was designed to be managed in a subluxation-centered chiropractic office and is an excellent cost effective marketing tool as well. If readers have additional questions about selling my books or how to manage this marketing program, I can be reached via email at *drjohnlreizer@gmail.com*. I will respond to any questions or comments submitted.

Utilize Testimonials

It is not uncommon for chiropractors to talk positively about the professional care they offer. After all, these business owners have a vested interest in pushing such services. Although patients will certainly gain some confidence in a doctor's ability to deliver competent care from listening to the claims of the practitioner, it is always more impressive for the healthcare consumer to hear and read positive comments coming from other satisfied patients.

There is probably no better way to convince prospects that your service is valuable than the use of testimonials. If you are not currently utilizing this marketing tool in your office, you should consider using testimonials from this day forward.

In order to be able to utilize testimonials, you need patients to begin making them. The question most doctors will ask is how do you actually get patients to give you positive feedback that can be used later on as a testimonial product? The answer is to simply ask patients to give you feedback about the services they have received. You need to ask patients if they wouldn't mind providing you with some comments about the professional services you have delivered and also if they would allow you to use the comments in the form of a testimonial.

I would also ask patients to sign a simple release statement when they create their comments about you. A sample letter and release might read like the example I have created below. Please feel free to copy or modify this template so that it suits your own needs.

Sample Letter & Release

Mrs. Sally Smith
My Happy Patient
Somewhere, USA

Dear Sally:

I would greatly appreciate it if you would take the time to offer me your candid opinion regarding my professional chiropractic services.

I would like to use your comments, with your permission, as a testimonial page in some of the marketing products I produce to promote my professional practice.

If this is agreeable, I would like for you to sign the very bottom of this letter authorizing me to publicly display your comments. I appreciate your kind consideration of my request.

Warmest regards,

John L. Reizer, D.C.

Patient's Signature_____ Date_____

Some Good Advice about Using Testimonials

It is important to only use original testimonials that are being generated from actual patients you are taking care of. Resist the urge to fabricate various testimonials on your behalf as they will probably not appear authentic to your prospects and existing patients.

Always make sure that you satisfy the **Health Insurance Portability and Accountability Act (HIPAA)** laws that are applicable. Once you have secured the patient's permission to use his or her comments, you can proceed and create your various testimonial presentations. I would use them in newsletters, office brochures, books that you might write and any other marketing concepts you can possibly think of. When you list the patient's name on the testimonial page, be sure to include the full name of the patient along with his or her town of residence. This gives the endorsement a better sense of authenticity.

When asking for testimonials, make sure you explain in your instructions that you would like for your patients to consider the following items when writing their thoughts on paper:

1. *Why did the patient initially need to see a chiropractor?*
2. *Why did the patient choose you over another practitioner?*
3. *How well did your professional care work for the patient?*
4. *What did the patient like the most about your professional care?*
5. *Can the patient create a summary statement about your care?*

Finally, ask the patient if you can attach his or her photograph to the testimonial page. I would neatly frame and hang the various testimonial products around the entire perimeter of your office which will produce a very impressive display for patients visiting you for professional services.

Utilizing testimonials on a regular basis will provide you with a very cost effective marketing tool. They will also create, in the minds of others, instant credibility for you as a professional healthcare provider within your immediate community.

Create a Community Greeting Program

Another cost effective marketing tool I regularly use in my private practice is a community greeting program. The concept is very simple and will help a doctor to market his or her professional services to people who have just moved into a new community.

There are a lot of businesses you can contact to help you get your program running efficiently. Simply go on the Internet and search for companies that specialize in collecting and selling mailing lists of new homeowners. The way the program operates is whenever a new home is sold or a person moves into the community where you have a practice, the person's mailing address is captured by the company you have retained and you are then forwarded a copy of the address. The chiropractor will then have an opportunity to send, to the new person, a community greeting letter inviting the resident to contact the doctor in the event he or she needs the services of a highly qualified chiropractor.

The cost of a marketing program which focuses on targeting new residents within a given community can run anywhere from $30 - $100 per month depending on the size of your community and the number of real estate transactions that have taken place each month. The effectiveness of a community greeting program will also obviously depend on a number of factors including the various materials you offer to the new members of the community.

I have included a sample copy of the letter I currently use which generates pretty consistent results each month. Please feel free to copy, modify and use this sample letter when implementing your own program within your private practice.

Dr. John L. Reizer
188 Blalock Road
Boiling Springs, SC 29316
864-494-0121

Dear Neighbor,

I would really like to take this opportunity to welcome you to the community of Boiling Springs, South Carolina. I know how exciting and intimidating it can be when a person decides to move his or her family, life and a collection of personal belongings to a new location.

I wanted to be one of the first business owners in our community to officially welcome you to the Upstate of South Carolina. I think you will find living in the Carolinas a great experience. We have a super little town that offers residents many amenities not commonly found in other communities. I encourage you to begin exploring your new home and to stop by to visit some of the businesses in the downtown area.

An important decision you will eventually have to make is locating a dependable doctor for your immediate family. This can be a daunting task and I know from many years of experience that most individuals do not like to make such a decision without the advice of a trusted friend who may know a local healthcare specialist. The problem however, is that you might not know a person who has firsthand experience with a healthcare specialist in our community. This is another reason I have decided to contact you. I wanted to introduce myself and my professional chiropractic services to you so that you can have a chance to see if I might be of professional assistance to you or the members of your family in the future.

Chiropractic is a safe, sensible and drug free way to maintain a healthy lifestyle. If you give me the chance to talk to you one on one, I would like to prove this to you. I can offer individual care for all members of your family. My chiropractic services are comprehensive and I can answer your health questions regarding lower back pain, sciatica, headaches, scoliosis, wellness care, as well as many other conditions.

I feel that you should be able to speak with a chiropractor one on one, to find out if your family would feel comfortable with a specific practitioner. Because I do feel this way, I would like to offer you and your family a free spinal exam so you can decide if the professional services I offer could directly benefit you.

If you would like additional information, please do not hesitate to call my office number which is 864-494-0121. I am always happy to answer any questions or schedule an appointment for new patients.

When you come in for your appointment, be sure to bring the special certificate that has been printed below with you. I really look forward to hearing from you.

Sincerely,
Dr. John L. Reizer
Chiropractor

Special Welcoming Certificate
COMPREHENSIVE CHIROPRACTIC CARE

This certificate entitles "new patients" to a
Free Spinal Screening and Consultation

Please call to make an appointment and present this certificate to:

Dr. John Reizer
Chiropractor
188 Blalock Road
Boiling Springs, SC 29316
864-494-0121

Offer Expires: _____

I believe when you utilize a community greeting program consistently over the course of many years, you will observe a nice influx of new patient appointments being scheduled at your office. This is a very cost effective marketing tool to use, and the best part is – it really works!

Market Wellness Care Services

One of the best ways for chiropractors to regularly attract new patients is to market professional *wellness care services*. Many chiropractors have become so caught up in the mainstream, condition-based treatment arena that they sometimes forget that regular chiropractic care will also provide patients with a great way to maintain their health naturally.

If doctors of chiropractic were to spend an adequate amount of time and energy marketing wellness care concepts to active patients as well as to potential prospects, they would gradually see a sizable increase in the number of new patients they processed on a monthly basis. Granted, this would take a little bit of work on the part of the doctors involved however, the end results would certainly more than compensate these practitioners for any additional sweat equity that might be required.

The advantages of marketing *wellness care services* are twofold. To begin with, patients who visit chiropractors for regular wellness checkups are motivated to maintain their care over a longer period of time. These patients are not looking to constantly opt out of a phase or plan of care just because their symptoms have changed. So much energy is commonly wasted by chiropractors when they routinely attempt to encourage practice members to follow through on various prescribed treatment plans.

When a group of patients become educated about the health benefits associated with lifetime care, this creates a winning situation for all parties involved. Patients obviously benefit because they are receiving more frequent care which promotes better overall body physiology. Chiropractors benefit tremendously as well because they are able to focus more clearly on providing quality care versus making sure patients are regularly compliant with care.

Secondly, chiropractors that are marketing *wellness care services* on a regular basis usually create a better understanding for patients, staff members, and associate doctors with regards to the value of chiropractic care in general. When a chiropractic practice becomes truly successful, it is because everyone involved with that practice possesses a collective understanding about the professional mission trying to be achieved in that unique setting. Understanding the value of chiropractic care is the first step in getting already established patients to refer new patients.

I indicated in an earlier chapter of this book, titled *"Create a Patient Referral Program,"* that doctors should always make the extra effort to teach their patients the importance of lifetime care. <u>I cannot over emphasize enough my belief that chiropractic should be explained to patients so that it is perceived by them as a sensible way to maintain health naturally</u>. If you are not currently marketing wellness care services to people in your community, then you or your office staff should definitely consider doing so in the near future.

It is also important for me to point out to readers that a marketing tool that is as valuable as this one is should never be overlooked by new or already established practitioners. It is never too early or too late to begin building a wellness clientele.

A final comment I would like to write about regarding this subject is that this marketing tool does not necessarily prevent a doctor or an entire practice from marketing more condition-based services at the same time. One marketing tool that focuses on *wellness care services* does not have to interfere with another marketing tool that is designed to attract prospects with specific conditions. Be creative and flexible when designing your marketing concepts and this will ultimately help your practice to grow.

Market Your Business During Leisure Activities

Great marketing concepts can be implemented at different times of the month. They do not have to be utilized exclusively when you are working in your professional practice. For many years I have been successfully marketing the different businesses I own during the hours I am taking part in leisure activities. One of the keys to having a successful marketing campaign is learning how to *"toot your own horn"* as often as possible and in any arena you might happen to find yourself in.

I regularly market the professional chiropractic services I offer during the hours I am away from the office. I routinely target the people who live in my immediate community with various marketing tools when I am out and about enjoying myself in a leisurely setting. In many instances I will accomplish this task by simply talking to people about one of my favorite subjects—chiropractic. It is never very difficult for me to work the subject of chiropractic into a conversation I might be having with various acquaintances. Sometimes, I will get the conversation rolling by making a statement such as, *"I just had one of the best days of work ever."* People will usually respond to this kind of talk with a raised eyebrow or even a general look of disbelief. Most people hate their jobs and are constantly counting the hours, minutes, and seconds remaining until the end of the work week. When they hear me make statements about how I enjoy the work I perform on a given day, they become very curious about why I often come across as being euphoric when discussing my occupation. They will usually ask me what I do for a living. This gives me the opening I require to make my move and before they can blink an eye, I am promoting my trade, its philosophy and of course the practice I own.

      I always market my businesses in a casual way so it is not perceived by others as being overbearing, but yet it allows people I am speaking with to understand how passionate I am about the work I perform. More importantly, it informs the people I am speaking with that I really believe the professional services I offer to be extremely important and valuable. The people who have dialogue with me usually come away from the conversations understanding a lot more about chiropractic and also about my business and the professional services it generates.

      Another way I often promote and market the businesses I own when I am away from the office is via the use of personalized license plates which are attached to both of the vehicles I drive. The personalized license plates display my practice website address. I also have professional looking magnetic signs on my car doors that advertise another business website. Some people might laugh at the way I go about trying to promote my businesses. In reality, my marketing efforts are able to draw a lot of positive attention to the services I offer. If and when I get stuck in a traffic jam I instantly become a billboard advertising campaign. I recently took a mini-vacation to the mountains and during the trip was locked in a traffic jam for about an hour. It was amazing to observe how many passengers in other vehicles were writing down my web address that was printed on the magnetic signs affixed to my car doors. These signs advertise a weight loss book I authored in January, 2008. When I returned home from my vacation, I noticed my web page had received over two hundred visitors and I sold fifty-five books. I was quite pleased about how effective this marketing tool worked while I was sitting in my car in a state of gridlock.

Another very clever way to market your business during leisure outings is to purchase T-Shirts with your company information prominently displayed on the front or back of the products. This is a very cost effective marketing tool to utilize and you can even hand them out to patients as gifts or prizes for referring you patients. If you decide to distribute the shirts to your patients, they will be able to help you market your professional services during the periods of time they are taking part in leisurely activities.

Finally, I believe it is important to get in the regular habit of carrying an ample supply of business cards on your person at all times. Whenever you pay a bill at a restaurant, write a check to a utility company, meet people on the street, or find yourself in a dozen other scenarios that will come your way, you should handout or distribute these marketing materials. The more business cards you give away, the better the chances will be that new patients will eventually come your way.

Set a personal goal to give out ten of your business cards every single day. That adds up over time. In one month you will have distributed 300 cards and in one year you will have given out approximately 3,600 business cards. Remember, business cards will be of little use to you if you leave them in a box collecting dust. The more often you circulate any of your marketing materials, the more likely the chances will be that your business will continue to grow.

Market Your Practice to other Professionals

As a chiropractor it will be necessary for you to regularly market your private practice to other professionals within your community. You should not limit the types of professionals you market your services to. The formation of relationships that ultimately lead to a well defined network of professionals that are willing to refer you patients on a regular basis will make it easier for you to build a successful practice with a high patient volume in the shortest period of time possible.

I would suggest that chiropractors market their services to dentists, neurologists, general medical practitioners, massage therapists, orthopedists, accountants, bankers, stock brokers, real estate agents and possibly some other local professionals. A group such as this will help practitioners to create a well diversified marketing/referral network.

A doctor should call a professional on the telephone after first writing a brief letter to him or her which introduces the doctor and the professional services he or she has to offer. The purpose of the phone call is to invite a specific professional out to lunch so the two professionals can get acquainted.

The lunch setting is a wonderful atmosphere to form a relationship with other people. This is a necessary step that must be taken in order that a chiropractor will be able to share important business related information with other professionals. A doctor should make sure to bring some business cards to the lunch date along with pertinent office related literature. Practitioners should also be prepared to explain to a lunch guest the value of their services and why it is important for the two professionals to regularly refer customers to one another. In order for this type of a relationship to work it will be important to establish the understanding that there will be mutual benefit achieved for both parties involved. A business referral relationship can only work over a sustained period of time if both professionals are willing to refer customers/patients on a regular basis. Also, the chiropractor should pay for the lunch.

Writing a Letter of Introduction

The first order of business you need to take care of is to write a really powerful letter of introduction which you will then obviously send to the various professionals you wish to market your professional service to. The sample letter that follows is a model you can use when constructing your own campaign. Please feel free to modify the sample document or you may use it exactly as it reads. In either scenario, the sample letter I have included should help readers create a powerful letter of introduction.

John Smith, M.D.
123 Hospital Drive
My Town, USA

Dear Dr. Smith

My name is Dr. John Reizer and I am a local chiropractor from Boiling Springs, SC. I would really love to have the opportunity to schedule a time where I could take you to lunch so that we could discuss how our professional services might be of mutual benefit to our existing patients. I know that we both have very busy schedules, but I really believe we should find the time to meet.

I will attempt to contact you by phone sometime early next week. I look forward to meeting you to learn about your professional services.

Talk soon,
John L. Reizer, D.C.
Chiropractor

When you send your letter, you should make sure that you mark on a calendar the date the document was mailed. Wait a few days and follow up your efforts with a phone call to the professional's place of business. It is important to speak politely and always maintain a very professional demeanor when discussing a possible lunch date. Once you have your lunch date scheduled, you should practice in front of a mirror what you want to say to your guest. Make sure you are able to clearly describe how your professional services can benefit that professional's patients, clients or customers.

When attending your luncheon, I recommend you dress professionally for the occasion. A nice suit and a tie are appropriate for such a meeting. You want to look the part of a professional and you want to convey to others that you are knowledgeable, experienced and proficient at what you do. Perception is everything and how you dress will help others to perceive you in a certain way.

Become a Good Listener

I believe it is extremely important to become a good listener when you are interacting with other professionals. People in almost every situation you can imagine love to talk about themselves and you must try to resist the strong urge to constantly talk about yourself. If you do your homework and are well prepared to present your business services, you will no doubt make a great impression each time you schedule a business lunch. This will allow you to regularly establish a number of long term relationships with many professionals in your community.

Once you have established a healthy referral network comprised of local professionals, you will be well on your way to building a very successful chiropractic practice that constantly receives an influx of new patients that are being referred from the local professionals within your community.

Market your Business on the Local News

In May, 2008 I was interviewed and featured on a local C.B.S. television affiliate in my community because of the weight loss book I authored. The news coverage I received was very helpful to my cause of selling books as the story created a lot of public awareness about my publication as well as the official website I created that is dedicated to promoting and selling the book. The C.B.S. story really boosted my book sales and it also helped me receive a lot of positive attention as a practicing chiropractor in my community.

Many of the faculty members that work with me at the chiropractic college where I am employed wanted to know how I was able to convince the local television station to do a story about my book. When I told them how I accomplished this feat, I think they were slightly disappointed with my answer. I believe they were expecting a very sophisticated explanation about how I presented my story to the news station and that in order to capture the attention of the editor I had to wait outside the television studio for weeks with my book in hand begging the person in charge for a chance to consider what I believed was a newsworthy story.

In reality, I was able to convince the studio to put me on television because I sent a copy of my book along with a cover letter and a copy of a press release *(you can view the actual document I submitted to the editor in the chapter that deals with writing press releases)* I had written months earlier to the station's health editor. I then followed up my initial letter submission with a couple of emails to the same person. At first I received no response from this editor. After about three or four weeks, I finally received a telephone call one morning at my home from her. The editor explained that she wanted to come to my residence in order to film an interview with me discussing my book. I immediately confirmed my availability to do such an interview and within a few hours the news crew arrived at my home with television cameras and microphones.

Later that evening the story ran on the six o clock evening news and my book was suddenly given tremendous exposure across the Upstate of South Carolina. I believe that several millions of people had an opportunity to learn about my publication. The best part of the entire event was that all of the publicity and news exposure was absolutely free. In addition to the media coverage being free, the news piece was also perceived by a large percentage of the viewing audience as being quite legitimate because the story was in the format of news and not in the format of an advertisement.

I have appeared many times throughout my professional career on television and radio programs. I have also been featured, for business related events, in news papers on numerous occasions. I have never paid a single dime to generate this type of publicity for any of the businesses I have been involved with. My ability to be able to regularly market the professional products/services I have offered over the past several years in the local media has provided me with a very cost effective marketing option that other doctors do not seem to take advantage of.

I believe the key to getting in the door to the local media is persistence on the part of the business owner. The people in the world who are persistent are usually the same people who end up becoming successful at whatever they are trying to accomplish. In the case of dealing with media companies, business owners have to maintain a very persistent attitude when submitting their products or services for consideration. Keep in mind that editors have to decide if what you are sending to them is newsworthy or not.

Once again, a strong and powerful cover letter is important when addressing an editor or reporter. In that letter you have to point out what makes your story different from competitors. Why would readers, listeners or viewers find a particular story interesting? It does not matter what the service is, you just have to dress it up so it is appealing to an editor.

Chiropractic services can easily be transformed into a newsworthy topic. Approach an editor and tell him or her you are interested in doing a talk show where listeners or viewers can call up and ask pertinent healthcare questions. This will be great for the radio or television station because it allows an audience to become interactive with a specific program. Although every service/product might not be headline news material, you can still manage to get on the air or featured in a news article via a talk show or in a question and answer newspaper column.

Use a sample cover letter such as the one I have included below to initiate a primary contact with a media company.

> *Dear Mr. Editor:*
>
> *I recently celebrated my 21st year as a practicing chiropractor in our local community. I have certainly had a wonderful career as a healthcare professional in the Upstate of South Carolina and I would like to have the chance to give something back to the people who have supported me for so many years.*
>
> *I was hoping that perhaps I could appear on your health show that is featured every Saturday morning. I have listened to the program often and always enjoyed the guests you invite on your show. In addition, the topics you choose are both interesting and informative at the same time.*
>
> *I feel that I also could offer some interesting and informative comments for your listeners and would very much like to do so. I have appeared on radio call in shows before and I have always been well received by the listening audience. Please find attached my resume and qualifications regarding my professional trade.*
>
> *If my proposal interests you, please contact me at your convenience so that we may explore together the possibility of bringing this type of a show to fruition. My contact information (business card) is enclosed as well.*
>
> *Best wishes,*
> *John Reizer, D.C.*

You might have to send a few follow up emails and perhaps a phone call or two to the editor. In the case of a radio or television show, the sound of your voice on the phone and how well your verbal skills are perceived by the show's producer can greatly help your case when trying to pitch your idea.

This is a great way to market you, your practice and the professional services you regularly offer to patients. Do not be bashful about contacting a talk show host. These people earn their paychecks by interviewing guests. If you come across as being confident, professional and someone who can offer some timely information about a current health topic, there is a very good chance you will end up getting booked on a show. Get out there right now and start marketing!

Create a Marketing Calendar

There is one final item that I have not yet mentioned in this book which is also extremely important to the success of any serious marketing campaign. In my opinion, a wide variety and healthy assortment of cost effective marketing tools will help you grow your professional chiropractic practice. The key however, to getting the best possible results out of a collection of marketing tools is learning how to organize and utilize them throughout the course of the year. This is accomplished best by the creation and utilization of a marketing calendar.

The creation and regular use of a marketing calendar has been essential in making my own marketing programs successful throughout the years I have been in business. A marketing calendar is not very difficult to build. I recommend readers purchase a three ring binder at any office supply store. Set up the binder so it has twelve different sections representing each month of the year. In each monthly section of the binder you should set up your marketing tools by writing down on paper the frequency timing and duration you have decided on for each of your marketing concepts. I get very specific when setting up my marketing tools and I break the month down into individual weeks. I am constantly arranging/scheduling a health talk seminar, a newspaper article, a writing project for a book, as well as other projects into my binder. After you work with your own marketing calendar for a little while, the actual process of setting up the binder will become easier to do.

In the very front of your binder you should also create an overview calendar that you can utilize as a quick reference tool in order to see what is scheduled during a given month/week. Please look at the sample calendar listed below:

MARKETING CALENDAR – 2019			
January:	**Week 1**	**Week 2**	**Week 3**
Week 4			
Submit talk show proposal to editor	Introduce yourself to 3 new businesses	Launch new office website	Prepare news article for February
February:	**Week 1**	**Week 2**	**Week 3**
Week 4			
Work on office newsletter	Submit book press release	In-office promotions begin	Community college course begins
March:	**Week 1**	**Week 2**	**Week 3**
Week 4			
Community greeting program	Health club campaign	Work on office testimonials	Wellness care campaign begins

This type of calendar will be helpful in keeping your various marketing tools more organized and will also ensure that you stick to the marketing campaign you design and develop. It is important to remember that your marketing program will only work for you if you make the effort to work on it. Most importantly, you have to stick to your plan for the entire year. A great amount of discipline is required for this type of program to work properly. If a practitioner becomes lazy or apathetic in regards to his or her marketing efforts, the overall business related results will certainly suffer.

Get in the habit of developing a simple but effective marketing calendar and then utilize this tool throughout the course of the year. This final product will help you to get the most out of every other marketing technique I have discussed in this book.

Afterword

I certainly hope that the ideas/concepts I have discussed in this book will be helpful to the members of our profession as they set out to design their own successful marketing campaigns. If my readers take the time to figure out what marketing techniques would be most effective for their own personalities, and then follow through by making a serious effort to develop and implement these techniques, I know they will be very pleased with the end results.

Marketing a business can be a lot of fun and it will also allow you to be an active participant in the constant development of your own business. Too many practitioners within our profession sit in their offices and just wait for patients to knock on the door. Granted, a fair number of new patients will walk into your office setting because they saw your sign from the road. This however, is not the best way to effectively build your livelihood. Be an active participant in growing your professional practice and learn from the very beginning that most of the tools that are required to grow a practice are quite cost effective and easily implemented into a new or already existing business model. You do not have to spend thousands of dollars each month to market your practice.

I hope you have enjoyed reading this book and I hope that I have made you aware of some pretty amazing chiropractic marketing tools that will absolutely grow your practice!

- Dr. John Reizer
  Chiropractor